This book presented to

_____

By

_____

on this day

_____

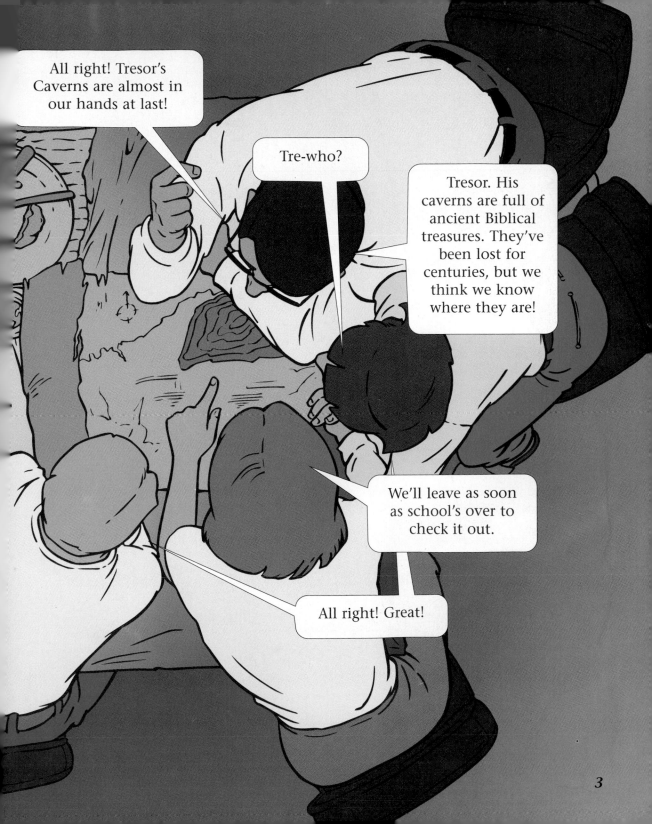

Acknowledgments

Concept and Storyline–
Rick Osborne

Concept Development–
Rick Osborne, Lightwave's
Creative Team, Jean Syswerda,
Gary Cleave

Art Director and Designer–
Terry Van Roon

Chief Illustrator–Chris Kielesinski

Writer–Christie Bowler

Production Manager–Ed Strauss

Airbrush Artist–Emilios Shiatis

Inker and Illustrator–Ken Save

Illustrator–Gerard deSouza

Desktop Publishing– Randy Arnold,
Beverly Arnold

Researcher–Phil Bowler

Editors–Jean Syswerda, Rick Osborne,
Sally Hupp, Elaine Osborne

Special thanks to Bibles International
of Canada for their significant
contribution to the project, and to
Andrew Jaster for his help with
desktop publishing.

Library of Congress Catalog Card Number: 96-61504

Published by Zondervan Publishing House
Grand Rapids, Michigan 49530, U.S.A.
http://www.zondervan.com

Printed in the United States of America

A Lightwave Production
P.O. Box 160 Maple Ridge
B.C., Canada V2X 7G1

97 98 99 4 3 2 1

4

The *Amazing* TREASURE BIBLE *Storybook*

ZondervanPublishingHouse
Grand Rapids, Michigan

A Division of HarperCollins Publishers

Character Sketches

Lori Delve–Adventurous archaeologist. Easily distracted. Full of life, enthusiasm and fun. "Let's do it!"

Josh Delve–Practical, organized archaeologist. Inventor. Detail man. Loves laughing and figuring things out. "What if we . . .?"

Christopher Delve–12. Thinker. Never gets lost. Soft heart. Thinks his sister is great! "Let me think . . ."

Nikole Delve–10. Spunky. Acts first. Wears her emotions on her sleeve. Good-hearted. Thinks Chris is the best! "Come on!"

Jamal Franklin–almost 13. Chris's best friend. Adventurous. Hands-on guy. Power-dives into the grass just to see what it's like. "Check it out!"

Madame Nadra Zamar–Kind-hearted. Gracious. Owns the land the castle and camp are on. Loves people. "Make yourself at home."

Zareef Zamar–Madame's cousin. Castle caretaker. Scholar. Jolly and warm. Mysterious. Always has a smile. "What do you think?"

Digger–Delve's family dog. Digging is his life! Has a nose for the unusual. Archaeologist in training. "Woof!"

Simianne–Zareef and Madame Zamar's monkey. Curious. Always grooming someone. Smarter than she looks. Loves to talk.

Table of Contents

How will we find Tresor's Caverns?

Well, they've been lost for centuries, so they're probably buried in rubble.

THE NEW TESTAMENT

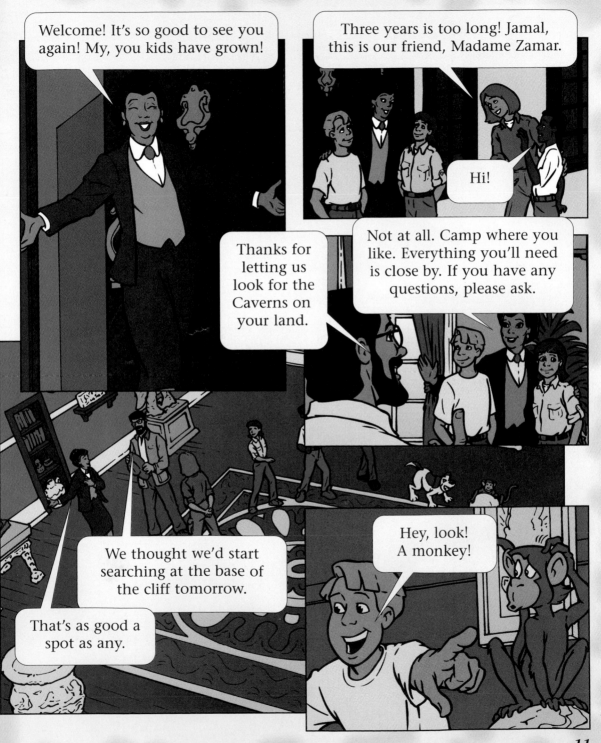

11

The ancient castle was perched on the highest ground for miles around, giving it a perfect view of the area. It looked mysterious in the afternoon light, its gray and purple walls silhouetted against the clear blue sky. A path wound up the hillside to the castle gate, set between two towers. A corner tower and the walls near it were crumbling, but the rest of the castle looked as solid as if it had grown right out of the rock.

The massive gate dwarfed the group as they approached. Just as they reached it a balding, bearded head popped through a doorway in one of the gate towers. "Ah, good! You came. Greetings! You remember old Zareef? Of course, yes. And these are your children? It has been too many years," Zareef grinned at them.

"It's good to see you again, old friend," Dad exclaimed, shaking the older man's hand vigorously. "These are our children, Chris and Niki. And this is Jamal."

"Woof!"

"And Digger," Dad laughed.

"Welcome! Welcome!" Zareef said. The monkey jumped from Madame Zamar's shoulder to Zareef's. "You have met Simianne? Good. What brings you here?"

"We're hunting for Tresor's Caverns," Mom answered. "We want the kids to discover just how real the Bible is. The things in Tresor's Caverns would do that!"

"Exactly! That is what they were for, yes?" Zareef agreed. "The Bible is the most real book in the world," he added.

"What do you mean?" asked Jamal.

"It is God's book. He gave it to us," Zareef explained. "He is very real and his book is like him. It affects all of life."

"God wrote a book?" Niki asked, surprised.

"Not the way you're thinking," Dad chuckled. "He used more than 40 people–shepherds and kings, prisoners and generals, doctors and tax collectors–who lived in different countries and different centuries to write the 66 books of the Bible. And the books all agree with each other. Together they tell one complete story. Only God could make a book like that!"

"The Bible has exciting truths and mysteries beyond counting!" Zareef exclaimed. "It tells us about God and how we can know him personally."

"And God is Truth," Mom added, "so his book is true."

"Awesome!" Jamal said. "Like this castle."

Dad laughed. "In a very different way."

"Can we look around?" Chris asked.

"Of course!" Madame Zamar said.
"Zareef, would you give us the tour?"

"Yes, yes. Come with me." Zareef
led them through the gate's archway
and into the main courtyard.

The whole castle was made of
large stone blocks. The same stone,
tightly fit together, made a solid,
even floor beneath their feet.

As Zareef showed the group around the castle, he explained, "This castle was built long ago by the Crusaders, Christian knights who fought to free the Holy Land from the Muslims. Since then, many rulers have lived here and added towers and rooms. Most of the castle has been kept in good repair. It is quite safe." He smiled and winked. "There is as much to explore here as you like."

Zareef led them across a large courtyard. It was open to the sky with several shade trees growing in he corners. A fish pond on one side sparkled in the afternoon sun. Digger lapped from the pond then followed everyone down some stairs into a square room with beautifully carved walls. It was cool and dark after the bright sunshine. In the center of the room a magnificent 20-foot column rose from a carved stone base.

"Ooh, look at that," Niki breathed. "It's gorgeous!"

"This column is the key to the castle," Zareef said with another wink at the kids. They all stared up at it. Its top looked like a tulip bud holding a stone cushion. Rising from the cushion was a cross. "Objects like this, and these wall carvings, were used to tell stories because not many people could read," Zareef explained. "Books were rare. Few people had their own Bibles."

"Bibles were rare?" Jamal asked.

Dad nodded. "There were only handwritten copies made carefully on papyrus, an ancient paper made from reeds, or parchment, which was made from leather."

"But," Chris asked, "how do we know they copied it right?"

"We have many pieces of very old copies of the Bible," Madame Zamar said. "Scholars compare them to see how closely they match. The differences are very few and very minor."

"Not far from here," Dad added, "old copies of the Bible, the Dead Sea Scrolls, were found. They were made nearly two thousand years ago, yet they're almost exactly the same as the Bibles we have today! It's been copied accurately, all right!"

"God made certain we have precisely what he wants!" Zareef concluded.

"Absolutely!" Mom agreed excitedly. "And archaeology keeps confirming what the Bible says. For a time, people didn't believe the Philistines were real. Imagine! But we've found masks and pottery they used. They were real, for sure! That's why we love archaeology!"

"And that's why we're here," Dad said with a grin. "Thanks for the tour, Zareef, Madame. We'd like to look around more. But right now we need to set up camp before it gets dark."

"Come and explore the castle any time, children," Zareef said.

"Thanks. We will!" the kids chorused, waving. Simianne waved back and chattered at them from Zareef's shoulder.

The Delves, Jamal and Digger made their way down the hill to the valley below, talking excitedly. After a brief scan of the area they chose a campsite under some trees near the stream and set to work unpacking. The sleeping and supply tents were quickly set up. Tarpaulins would provide shade for cooking, eating and working areas. Another, smaller tent became a shower room. Digger dug his own sleeping hollow between the kids' tents.

As everyone worked they talked about the day. "The Bible sounds cool," Jamal said. "And really old!"

"It is. But it's important today too," Mom explained. "God made us.

That means he knows how we, and everything else, work best. The Bible explains it all. It's God's love letter to us, and it tells us how to live."

Later, after the camp was set up and organized, they all relaxed with hot chocolate before going to bed. Crickets chirped in the quiet night. They could hear the soft sound of the stream gurgling its way over and around rocks. A light breeze rustled the leaves overhead and played with their hair. Mom said softly, "This is so beautiful!" She sighed happily. "I just know we're close. Tresor's Caverns may be right under our feet. I can't wait to get started!"

"Can we explore the castle tomorrow?" Chris asked. Niki and Jamal hardly breathed as they waited for the answer.

"Why not?" Dad answered. "Zareef said it's safe. He'll be there if you need anything."

"Ooh, I can hardly wait!" Niki declared. "I won't sleep at all!"

"I guess we're all excited about our plans for tomorrow!" Mom laughed. "You know," she added thoughtfully, "God was excited about his plans too."

"God was excited?" Niki asked, surprised. "What plans?"

"He sure was!" Dad answered.

"The Bible is the story of God's one big plan for the human race–to make a way for people to join his family."

"God has a family?" Jamal inquired. He'd never thought of that before.

"He sure does. The Bible explains it to us. It also tells us what God is like," Mom added. "He cares about us and answers when we ask for help. He's holy and pure."

"He's everywhere even though we can't see him, right?" Chris asked.

"Right. He sees and knows everything. He can do anything," Dad answered.

"And he loves us!" Niki said with a grin. "That's my favorite!"

"Mine too," Mom agreed. "It's all in his book, Jamal. Maybe we can read it together while we're here."

"Sounds great," Jamal grinned. Then he yawned sleepily.

Dad laughed, "I agree, Jamal. It's been a long day. Bedtime. Tomorrow–explorations!"

The next morning at the castle.

23

The kids and Simianne found themselves at the end of one arm of a huge cross-shaped room. They entered cautiously. Their footsteps echoed back from the stone walls and marble pillars as they began exploring. Light from skylights and high, narrow windows lit the room. It smelled faintly of polish and old paper. Dust danced in the air. The room was filled with bookshelves, statues, models of gardens and buildings, paintings, stained glass pictures, tapestries, columns, ancient scrolls, strange objects, murals, carvings and suits of armor!

Right in the center of the room, where the two arms of the cross met, a large metal globe taller than the kids rose from the stone floor. Maps, symbols and pictures were engraved on it. More symbols and pictures were chiseled into the stone of the floor all around it. From the

globe they could see down all four wings of the room, three short ones about the same length and one much longer.

"Ohh!" Niki breathed. "We've landed in a dream or something."

Chris looked around in astonishment. "This place is awesome! Secret passages and treasure. You guys were right!"

"But I don't see any treasure," Niki protested. "I mean there aren't any piles of jewels or gold and stuff."

"I wonder . . . Hey!" Chris said, "What if those words in the hallway are a clue?"

"You mean . . . we have to 'know his plan,' like it said, to find the treasure?" Jamal asked excitedly. "A treasure hunt. All right!"

"Look!" Chris pointed at the ceiling. The central skylight looked like it was under water. "The fishpond!" he exclaimed. "Wow, I never would have guessed! We walked right by it."

"Look at this," Niki called. She was staring up at mobiles of solar systems like the ones in her science class at school. On the floor beneath them, at the corner where two of the short wings met, was a model of a garden. A beautiful, realistic tree almost as tall as Niki stood to one side. "It's like the Garden of Eden or something," Niki murmured. "Chris, the Bible starts with, 'In the beginning,' right?" she asked. "Like on the door?"

"You're right, Niki. The verse on the column was from the Bible too. And the Treasure Bible opened the door. Hmm. Let me think . . ." Chris's voice faded away. Simianne scratched her head as if she were thinking too.

"Read the 'In the beginning' stuff from the Bible, Chris," Jamal suggested, "Maybe it's another clue or something. This is great!"

"Yeah!" Chris exclaimed. "Hey, Dad said the Bible was the story of God's plan. We're onto something!" Chris opened the Treasure Bible and read.

Creation

(Genesis 1–2)

In the beginning, God created the heavens and the earth. The earth didn't have any shape. And it was empty.

God spoke and whatever he said came into being. He made light and dark. He made the stars, sun and moon. He made the land and the seas. And he made every kind of plant that grows.

At that time, the LORD God hadn't sent rain. But streams came up from the earth. They watered the whole surface of the ground.

The LORD God planted a garden in the east, in Eden. He made all kinds of trees grow out of the ground. Their fruit was good to eat. The tree that gives life forever was in the middle of the garden. The tree that gives the ability to tell the difference between good and evil was also there. A river watered the garden.

Then God made creatures to live in this wonderful place. He formed all of the wild animals and the birds of the air out of the ground. He made all kinds of creatures that move along the ground. He made all the fish and every other living being.

God saw everything he had made. And it was very good.

"God made everything? Whoa!" Jamal said as he examined the garden.

"Yeah. He can do anything!" Chris added, closing the Bible.

"Hey, if this is like the Garden of Eden," Niki suggested, "maybe this is the tree of life. Or the tree for telling the difference between good and evil."

"Then it should be in the middle," Jamal declared. "Help me, Chris!"

The boys pushed the miniature tree toward the center of the model garden. It moved smoothly along a track they hadn't noticed before. As it reached the center of the little garden a low rumbling sound came from the wall behind them.

Simianne squealed and dove for Niki's shoulder. Part of the wall had a painting of a man and woman on it and it was moving backward, like a doorway. When the movement stopped, an archway opened into another room.

The kids looked at each other. Suddenly Jamal grinned. "Another secret room! Maybe that's where the treasure is." He ran for the opening. "Let's check it out!"

"This place is amazing!" Chris agreed as he moved toward the archway. "You know what? This Bible seems to be the key to all this stuff. We'd better hang on to it! Come on!"

Simianne clung to Niki's shoulder as she followed the boys through the opening. Narrow windows high in the walls near the entrance lit the near end of the long, rectangular room. Its walls were covered in a colorful, peaceful mural of the Garden of Eden. Every imaginable animal, bird and plant was painted in vivid color. There were varieties the kids had never seen or even dreamed of before.

They moved into the room to examine the mural, pointing out strange animals and exotic birds and plants to each other. The farther they went into the long room, the darker it got.

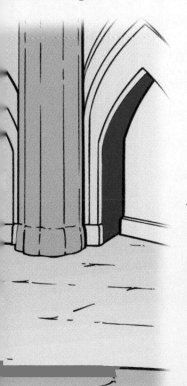

"Well, no jewels or treasure," Jamal stated, looking around. "Who are they?" He pointed to the two people in the picture.

"They must be Adam and Eve," Chris answered. "They were the first human beings. We didn't read that part yet."

"The first people? Cool. I wonder if they really looked like that," Jamal said, his head to one side.

"I doubt it," Chris laughed. "That's just someone's idea of what they might have looked like."

"Aren't they why God made the garden? I mean he made it for them, right?" Niki asked.

"I think so," Chris answered. "Here, I'll read about it."

How Old is it?

Only God knows how old the earth really is. Some people think it's billions of years old. Other people disagree and say the earth is only a few thousand years old. Whatever the age of the earth is, we know one thing for sure: God created the world and everything in it.

Verse: Genesis 1:1
"In the beginning, God created the heavens and the earth."

Adam and Eve in the Garden

(Genesis 1–2)

After God had made everything, he said, "Let's make human beings in our likeness." So God formed a man out of the dust of the ground. He breathed the breath of life into him. And the man became a living person.

God put the man in the Garden of Eden. He commanded, "You can eat the fruit of any tree in the garden. But you mustn't eat the fruit of the tree of the knowledge of good and evil. If you do, you will die."

Then God said, "It's not good for the man (Adam) to be alone. I'll make a helper just right for him."

So God caused Adam to sleep. While he was sleeping, God took out one of his ribs and closed up the opening. Then the LORD God made a woman. He made her from the rib. He brought the woman (Eve) to Adam.

So God created human beings in his own likeness.

God blessed them. He said, "Have children and increase your numbers. Fill the earth and bring it under your control."

Adam and Eve looked after the Garden. They were happy and peaceful. They enjoyed God's love as his children. Until one day . . .

Adam and Eve Sin

(Genesis 3)

Satan, an important angel who became God's enemy, disguised himself as a snake. He didn't want Adam and Eve to be with God and obey him. He said to Eve, "Did God really say, 'You mustn't eat the fruit of any tree in the garden'?"

Eve said, "God did say, 'You must not eat the fruit of the tree in the middle of the garden. If you do, you'll die.'"

"You won't die," Satan said. "You'll be like God."

Eve saw that the fruit was good to eat. And it would make a person wise. So she took some of the fruit and ate it. She also gave some to her husband, who was with her. And he ate it.

Suddenly, they were afraid. They hid from God when he came to the garden. They had disobeyed him. That's sin. So God sent them out of the Garden of Eden and away from him. Because they were the first people, everyone born since then has been born sinful, outside of God's presence. But God had a plan to bring people back to him. He hinted at it by saying a descendant of Eve's would crush the snake's head.

"God sent Adam and Eve away!" Jamal said.

"But they didn't die like they were supposed to!" Niki exclaimed. "Man! What did they go and eat the fruit for?"

"I guess they thought they knew better than God," Chris suggested. "Satan lied to them."

"Yeah. He always lies," Niki agreed. "That's the saddest story in the Bible, *I* think! Being separated from God is the absolute worst!"

Chris agreed, "It's almost like dying. Hey! Maybe that's it, Niki. Maybe they kind of died."

"Look, the whole story's right here!" Jamal said suddenly. He had been examining the walls farther from the door. "This mural shows everything Chris just read about."

"Here's where God sent them away," Niki pointed. She moved back to get a better look and stepped on a stone. "Look out!" she yelled as the stone moved under her foot and a low rumbling began. Simianne squealed. A solid wooden wall rose from the floor behind them, blocking them off from the entrance to the main room and leaving them in the dark.

"What happened?" Niki said. "Chris? Where are you?"

"Right here. Don't worry, Niki. Look, there's a bit of light coming from that tiny window." Chris groped for Niki's hand and led her toward the small shaft of light.

"Something came out of the floor right beside me," Jamal said. "Boy, did I jump!" As their eyes adjusted to the gloom they saw that a large bronze snake, poised to strike, had risen from the floor in the corner farthest from the new wall.

"Ooh, ugly!" said Niki, getting her courage back. "Like the snake in the story. I wonder if this is what it was like when God sent Adam and Eve away."

"Yeah, me too. Gotta ask Mom and Dad about that one," Chris agreed. "If we ever get out of here," he added in a whisper. More loudly he said, "If we come back tomorrow I vote we bring flashlights."

"Good idea," Jamal agreed. "You know," he added, "the story you read sounded like Eve's kid would get the last laugh on the snake. Crushing his head and all."

"You're right, Jamal," Chris responded. "Dad says that verse is a promise about Jesus. It's all part of God's plan."

"God's plan?" Niki said excitedly. "It's a clue! We're hot on the trail! When we figure this out maybe it'll lead us to the treasure!"

"Yeah!" Jamal agreed. "Read the next part, Chris." Chris held the Treasure Bible in the shaft of light and began to read.

Location of Eden

Hey! Two of the rivers, the Tigris and Euphrates, that Genesis 2 says "flowed out" of the Garden of Eden now "flow out" of the highlands of the modern-day country of Turkey. That means the Garden of Eden was probably in Turkey. How about that!

Verse: Romans 3:23
"Everyone has sinned. No one measures up to God's glory."

35

Cain and Abel

(Genesis 4)

Adam and Eve had two sons, Cain and Abel. One day Cain gathered some of the crops he'd grown. He brought them as an offering to the LORD. But Abel brought the fattest parts of some of the lambs from his flock. They were the male animals born first to their mothers. The LORD was pleased with Abel and his offering. But he wasn't pleased with Cain and his offering. So Cain became very angry.

God loved Cain. He spoke to him. "Why are you angry? Do what's right. Then you'll be accepted."

But Cain wouldn't listen. He attacked his brother Abel and killed him.

The LORD said to Cain, "Where's your brother Abel?"

"I don't know," he replied. "Am I supposed to look after my brother?"

But God knew what Cain had done and punished him for his sin.

This murder was just the beginning of the evil things people would do because they were separated from God. As the number of people grew, they did whatever evil things they wanted instead of obeying God.

Years later, out of all the people in the world, only one man pleased God.

Noah and the Ark

(Genesis 6–7, 9)

The LORD saw how bad the sins of all people had become. He was very sad that he'd made human beings. His heart was filled with pain.

But the LORD was pleased with Noah, a godly man, without blame. So he said to Noah, "Make yourself an ark. I'm going to bring a flood on the earth. Everything on earth will die. Enter the ark with your family. Bring two of every living thing into the ark, male and female. They'll be kept alive with you."

Noah did everything exactly as God commanded him.

When the birds and animals were in the ark, it rained. For 40 days the flood kept coming. Every living thing that moved on the earth died. And so did every human being. Only Noah and those with him in the ark were left.

When the waters went down God made a special promise to Noah. He said, "I am making my covenant with you and with all who'll be born after you. A flood will never destroy the earth again. I've put my rainbow in the clouds. It will be the sign of the covenant between me and the earth."

"An ark's a big boat, right? Imagine building something like that!" Jamal exclaimed. "Noah sure must have trusted God."

"Yeah!" Chris agreed. "That was God's second promise. The first was about crushing Satan's head. God gave them because he still loved people even though they sinned."

After a pause Niki asked, "How do we get out of here? Can you reach that window, Chris?"

"If I stand on the snake . . . Hey, standing on its head will be like crushing it!" Chris clambered up. "Yikes!" The snake tilted, dumping him onto the floor. Chris scrambled to his feet. "Uh-oh. Do you hear something?"

"Sounds like . . . *water*!" Jamal yelled. Water was pouring into the room through openings near the floor and halfway up the wall. Soon it was knee deep and still climbing.

"I think we're in trouble," Niki shouted. Simianne chattered angrily and leaped for the small window.

"It's like the flood! Look," Chris pointed to part of the wall mural. At chest level Noah's ark was perched on some mountains. "The ark was safe. Let's hope the water doesn't get any higher than that." The kids watched nervously as the water rose. Sure enough, it stopped just below the ark.

"Yes! I was right!" Chris exclaimed, splashing Jamal in his excitement. Jamal splashed back. A water fight broke out.

Holding the Bible above her head, Niki yelled, "Hey! Be careful! You'll get the Bible wet." When things calmed down Simianne jumped down from the window again. With Simianne out of the way, a shaft of light glinted off the water and danced across the ark in the mural.

"The ark saved Noah. I wonder . . ." Jamal waded across and pushed the ark's door. THUNK! "Yes!" The water drained out through the ground-level openings. When it was gone part of the mural slid aside. They went

Flood Stories

Some people think the flood never happened. But many countries around the world (like America, China, Egypt, Mexico and Greece) have stories, in their ancient histories, of a world-wide flood similar to the Bible's.

How could they all know about it separately unless it really happened?

Verse: Genesis 6:5-6
"The Lord saw how bad the sins of all people had become on the earth. All of the thoughts in their hearts were always directed only toward what was evil. The Lord was very sad that he had made human beings on the earth. His heart was filled with pain."

through the opening and found themselves in the large cross-shaped room again.

"Boy! Am I glad to see this place!" Chris exclaimed.

"That was wild! Is it lunch time yet?" Jamal asked.

"And do I have questions for Mom and Dad!" Niki added.

It was too early for lunch but they decided to head back anyway and dry off. They returned through the long hallway to the room with the column. The door to the outside was closed tight.

"Maybe we can't take the Bible out," Niki suggested. "What happens if we put it back?" Chris placed the Bible back onto the pedestal. It lifted up into its original position and the outside door opened with a click. Simianne left them as the kids rushed out and down the hill.

The kids found both parents busy at the dig near the base of the cliff. "You won't believe what we found!" Niki exclaimed. "Fantastic rooms and . . ."

"That's nice, dear," Mom said absently, examining some pottery.

Niki looked at Chris. He shrugged and grinned, "They're into pottery. You know what that means! Wait 'til we find the treasure."

Later, over lunch, Jamal inquired, "How come God sent Adam and Eve away after they ate the fruit?"

"Didn't God love them anymore?" Niki asked.

"Why didn't they die?" Chris added.

"One at a time," Dad laughed. "God still loved them. But he hates sin. It's sin that separates us from God. God is life. So when sin separates us from God, we die. Inside, in our spirits."

"Then why put the tree there in the first place?" Chris asked.

"God wanted Adam and Eve to love and obey him because they chose to, so he gave them a choice," Mom explained. "They chose to disobey. They didn't know how awful being separated from God would be."

"It's horrible!" Niki said, remembering the darkened room with the bronze snake. "It's dark and

scary and lonely."

Dad put his arm around her. "It sure is. Because Adam and Eve chose sin, everyone who came after them was born sinful and separated from God too."

"We can't be with God because of them?" Jamal asked. "That's not fair."

"It's not just because of them. We all sin when we do wrong. But don't worry. God had a plan to bring us back to him. The first part of the Bible sets up the problem. The rest is about getting God's plan ready and then putting it into action!"

"Good!" Jamal sighed. "I was getting worried–with the flood and all."

"The Bible has a great ending," Mom said. "But things were pretty bad at first. God destroyed everything because people were so evil. He had to show that sin has serious results." Curious, she asked, "Why all the questions?"

"We've been reading Genesis," Chris explained.

"Did you get to the story of Abraham?" Dad asked. When they shook their heads he continued, "He'll be next. Say! There's a Bedouin camp nearby. They live a lot like Abraham did. Let's head over there!" The kids agreed eagerly.

The Bedouins welcomed their visitors and kindly showed them around. Their houses were tents made of goat-hair cloth. They introduced the family to their goats and even gave them camel rides! They knew who Abraham was and chatted eagerly with the family about him. To answer the kids' curiosity Dad pulled out the battered Bible he always carried and started reading.

You'll Surely Die!

Life comes from God. Jesus said he was the Way, the Truth and the Life. Sin separates us from God. Without God we die on the inside, in our spirits. That's why the result of sin is death. God's plan makes a way to pay for our sins so we can be with him and alive in our spirits again. That's called being "born again."

Verse: Romans 5:12
"Sin entered the world because one man sinned. And death came because of sin. Everyone sinned, so death came to all people."

Abraham and Sarah

(Genesis 12, 15, 17)

Noah's family grew until, many years later, there were lots of people in the world again. God chose a man named Abram for the next part of his plan.

He hinted about the plan. He said, "Leave your country and your people. Go to the land I'll show you. All nations on earth will be blessed because of you."

Abram obeyed.

Then the LORD took Abram outside and said, "Look up at the sky. Count the stars, if you can. That's how many children you'll have."

Abram believed the LORD. The LORD accepted Abram because he believed. So his faith made him right with the LORD.

The LORD made a covenant with Abram. He said, "I'm giving this land to your children after you."

God chose Abram's wife, Sarah, too. He said, "I'll give her my blessing. I'll give you a son by her. I'll bless her so she'll be the mother of nations. Kings of nations will come from her."

God changed Abram's name to Abraham. He was 100 years old. Sarah was 90. They were too old to have children, but God kept his promise and did a miracle. He gave them a baby, Isaac.

Isaac

(Genesis 22)

Abraham and Sarah loved their son Isaac.

Some time later God put Abraham to the test. God said, "Take your son, the one you love, Isaac. Give him to me as a burnt offering. Sacrifice him on one of the mountains I'll tell you about."

God wanted to see how much Abraham trusted him.

Abraham put the wood for the burnt offering on his son Isaac. He himself carried the fire and the knife. The two of them walked on

together. Isaac didn't understand what was happening. "The fire and wood are here," he said. "But where's the lamb for the burnt offering?"

Abraham answered, "God himself will provide the lamb."

When they reached the place, Abraham built an altar and got ready to sacrifice Isaac. But God stopped him. Abraham looked up. He saw a ram caught in a bush nearby and sacrificed it instead.

The angel of the LORD called out to Abraham. "Now I know you have respect for God. You haven't held back from me your only son. I am taking an oath in my own name. I will certainly bless you. All nations on earth will be blessed because of your children. All because you have obeyed me."

The family thanked their hosts for their hospitality. Talking excitedly they headed back through the dusk to their own camp. The aroma of goats and camels followed them, carried on the warm evening breeze.

"I could live like them!" Niki said later, as they cleaned up after supper. "Traveling on camels is fun. But," she added, "I'd miss our big TV."

"When you carry everything, smaller is better," Dad agreed. "Speaking of technology, I've adapted a couple of mini-phones to work here. Take one with you tomorrow so we can keep in touch."

"And take a lunch," Mom suggested. "Then you can explore to your hearts' content. Just be back before dark. Abraham trusted God to take care of his son. I think we can trust you'll be OK at the castle."

"Did Abraham know God would save Isaac?" Jamal asked.

"He believed God's promise to make Isaac into a nation," Dad

explained. "So he trusted God to do that, no matter what. It's important to trust God, even when you don't understand how things will work out."

"Abraham knew God," Mom explained. "It's easier to trust people we know. That's why we should get to know God. Now," she added, "to bed."

The next morning, with mini-phone, lunches and flashlights in Niki's backpack, the kids returned to the castle. Simianne joined them as they retrieved the Treasure Bible and went to what they called the Globe Room.

Jamal glanced at the ceiling. "Look, stars! Maybe we should count them like Abraham did." But there were too many!

"What was important about the Isaac story?" Chris wondered. "The sacrifice? The lamb?"

"There's a lamb!" Niki pointed to the floor beside the globe.

Jamal ran to look. As he leaned on the globe it rotated under him. "It moves!" he shouted. He set it

spinning then dove onto it and got a ride. "Wheee!"

They all took turns riding the globe. Even Simianne. Then Chris exclaimed, "Look! Another lamb! Here on the globe! What if we matched them up?" They rotated the globe until the two lambs matched exactly. After a couple seconds they heard a THUNK! and a nearby bookshelf rotated outward. In the opening behind it hung a tent-like canvas.

"Like the Bedouins' camp! Or Abraham's!" Jamal called. The kids ran for the opening and found a room made up like the Bedouin camp. Tapestries, like fancy tent walls, told the story of Abraham and Isaac. At the far end of the room two doors were labeled "Esau" and "Jacob."

"They're Bible guys!" Chris declared. "Let's read about them."

Sacrifices

Whenever a Hebrew family offered sacrifices to God it was like a lesson! The parents used sacrifices to teach their children that there's no forgiveness of sins possible without sacrifice. That's because the Bible says the penalty for sin is death. Something or someone has to die to pay for sin.

Verse: Hebrews 9:22
"In fact, the law requires that nearly everything be made clean with blood. Without the spilling of blood, no one can be forgiven."

50

Jacob and Esau

(Genesis 25, 27)

Isaac grew up and got married. He prayed for his wife, Rebekah, because she couldn't have children. She had twins, Esau first, and then Jacob. Before they were born God chose Jacob for his plan.

Fathers used to pray a blessing for their oldest son. But Rebekah loved Jacob. She wanted him to get the blessing. When Isaac was old and blind, Rebekah helped Jacob steal the blessing from Esau. One day, when Esau was out hunting, she prepared some tasty food just the way Isaac liked it. She took the best of Esau's clothes and put them on Jacob. She covered his hands with the skins of the goats. (Esau was hairy.) Then she handed Jacob the tasty food and the bread she had made.

Jacob pretended to be Esau.

Jacob went close to his father. Isaac touched him and said, "The voice is the voice of Jacob. But the hands are the hands of Esau." Isaac didn't recognize him. His hands were covered with hair like those of Esau. So Isaac gave Jacob his blessing.

Then Esau brought food to his father. He begged Isaac to bless him too. But it was too late.

Jacob's Family

(Genesis 33, 35, 37)

Esau was very angry with Jacob. So Jacob ran away to his uncle. He worked there many years and married Leah and Rachel. He had twelve sons (Reuben, Simeon, Levi, Judah, Dan, Naphtali, Gad, Asher, Issachar, Zebulon, Joseph and Benjamin) and a daughter, Dinah.

After twenty years Jacob decided to return home. On the way God changed his name to Israel and blessed him. After a long journey, one day Jacob looked up. There was Esau! Jacob was nervous about meeting Esau again. But Esau ran to meet Jacob. He threw his arms around his neck and hugged him.

Jacob came home to his father Isaac, near where Abraham and Isaac had stayed. Isaac lived 180 years. Then he took his last breath and died. He was very old when he joined the members of his family who had already died. His sons Esau and Jacob buried his body.

Joseph was 17 years old. Israel (Jacob) loved Joseph more than any of his other sons. Joseph had been born to him when he was old. Israel made him a beautiful robe. Joseph's brothers saw that their father loved him more. So they hated Joseph. They couldn't even speak one kind word to him.

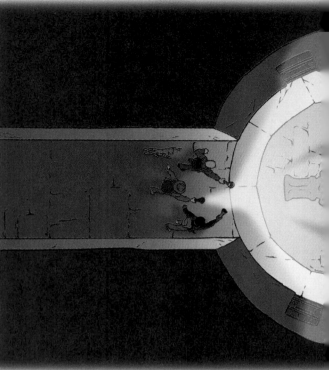

Chris frowned as he closed the Treasure Bible. "The blessing should have been Esau's! I vote for the Esau door."

"I'm with you," Jamal agreed. Together they opened the door marked 'Esau' and stepped through. Immediately water squirted them from all directions!

"Yow! Cold!" Jamal yelled as he twisted and turned to avoid the water.

"Now I know what a car in a car wash feels like," Chris said, jumping back through the open doorway. Simianne leaped out of his way. She sounded like she was giggling as she jumped for Jamal's shoulder.

"Guess that's the wrong door," Niki laughed. "The only other choice is Jacob. But he cheated."

Jamal was thinking about what they had read, "Maybe we have to go with who God chose. You know, trust him, like your parents said."

Niki remembered the mini-phone and fished it out of her backpack. "Let's ask Mom and Dad," she suggested. She spoke into the small phone, "Hey, Mom, can you hear me?" The boys crowded around to hear. "How come God chose Jacob, not Esau. Jacob was a thief!"

Mom's voice came through the tiny speaker. "God chooses people

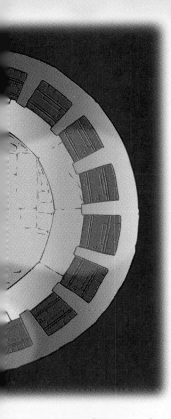

because he wants to, not because they deserve it," she replied. "He doesn't look at things like we do. He knew Jacob was the man he needed for his long-term plan."

"Oh, I see. Thanks," Niki said as she hung up.

"Well, who's going to open the Jacob door?" Jamal asked. They discussed it and decided to do it together, cautiously. Simianne clung to Jamal. The door opened easily into a stone hallway that led to an empty circular room. The shape of a menorah, the seven-branched Israelite candlestick, was inlaid with rounded stones in the floor of the room. The kids shone their flashlights around. The light revealed twelve evenly spaced doors. Each door was labeled with the name of one of Jacob's sons. The kids opened a couple but found only tiny dark rooms behind them.

"Hey, this door's marked 'Joseph.' He was Jacob's favorite son!" Chris exclaimed as he pulled on the handle. The door opened into a softly lit, rectangular room with two sections. The main part had couches and piles of plump pillows and soft blankets. It was rich and comfortable. The smaller section resembled a prison cell. It was dark; iron bars surrounded it and old straw covered the floor. On the wall between the two sections was one word: "Choose!"

"Yuck! Who'd choose that one?" Niki asked, pointing to the cell.

"I don't know, but we've been wrong before," Jamal remarked, diving into the pile of pillows. "Read some more, Chris. Maybe there'll be a clue."

Joseph's Family Line

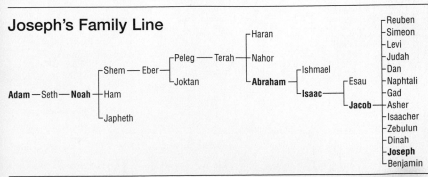

Adam — Seth — **Noah**
- Ham
- Shem — Eber
  - Peleg — Terah
    - Haran
    - Nahor
    - **Abraham**
      - Ishmael
      - **Isaac**
        - Esau
        - **Jacob**
          - Reuben
          - Simeon
          - Levi
          - Judah
          - Dan
          - Naphtali
          - Gad
          - Asher
          - Isaacher
          - Zebulun
          - Dinah
          - **Joseph**
          - Benjamin
  - Joktan
- Japheth

Verse: John 15:16
"You did not choose me. Instead, I chose you. I appointed you to go and bear fruit. It is fruit that will last. Then the Father will give you anything you ask for in my name."

Joseph, the Dreamer

(Genesis 37, 39)

One morning, Joseph said to his brothers, "Listen to the dream I had. We were tying up bundles of grain. Suddenly my bundle stood up. Your bundles gathered around my bundle and bowed down to it."

They said, "Will you really rule over us?" So they hated him even more because of his dream.

One day Joseph went to the fields to see his brothers. They saw him coming and decided to get rid of him. They tore his beautiful robe and

sold him to traders going to Egypt. They convinced their father that Joseph was dead.

The traders sold Joseph to Potiphar, one of Pharaoh's officials. Joseph's master saw that the LORD gave Joseph success in everything he did. So Potiphar put Joseph in charge of his house.

After a while, his master's wife noticed Joseph. She wanted him to love her. But he said, "No. My master trusts me. You're his wife. So how could I do an evil thing like that? How could I sin against God?"

One day she grabbed Joseph. But he ran away. When Potiphar came home, she lied, saying Joseph had tried to hurt her.

Joseph's master became very angry. So he put Joseph into prison.

Joseph, the Egyptian Ruler

(Genesis 42, 45–46, 50)

Pharaoh, Egypt's king, dreamed that seven skinny cows ate seven fat cows. He heard that Joseph understood dreams. So Joseph was brought from prison. God told Joseph the dream meant seven years with lots of food, then seven without food–a famine.

Joseph gave Pharaoh a plan to make sure there was enough food. Pharaoh liked it so much he put Joseph in charge of it. Joseph became the most important man in Egypt next to Pharaoh.

Later, during the famine, Israel's family needed food. Joseph's brothers went to Egypt to buy grain. When they arrived, they bowed down to Joseph. Joseph recognized them, but they didn't recognize him. Then Joseph remembered his dreams about them.

At first he pretended not to know them. Later he said to his brothers, "I'm your brother Joseph, whom you sold into Egypt. Don't be afraid. You planned to harm me. But God planned it for good. He wanted to save many lives."

When Israel heard Joseph was alive he was thrilled. God spoke to him, "Don't be afraid to go to Egypt. There I'll make you into a great nation. I'll go with you. I'll bring you back again."

Israel and Joseph met again in Egypt.

"All that talk about food makes me hungry," Jamal declared. The others agreed, so they got out their lunches and ate as they talked, feeding bits to Simianne.

"Joseph sure had it rough," Niki said. "But it turned out great! God had a plan for him. And he got back with his dad in the end."

"Yeah, he trusted God," Chris added. "Remember Mom said it's hard to trust? Joseph must have known God would come through for him."

"Do you think God has plans for us too?" Jamal asked.

"I hope so," Niki replied. "Hey! Look!" she pointed to a pedestal hidden among the pillows. "It's like the one upstairs that we get the Bible from."

"Maybe we're supposed to put the Bible on it," Jamal suggested. Chris laid the Treasure Bible on the top of the pedestal. Nothing happened. "There's one in the jail too!" Jamal pointed to a shadowed corner of the cell. They moved to the prison cell and Chris placed the Bible on that pedestal. CLANG! Bars like a cage door dropped into place behind them.

"Uh-oh," Niki said. "This doesn't look good."

"Maybe we'll be in prison a while

before something good happens," Chris guessed. "Like Joseph."

"Yeah. It worked for him," Jamal added, testing the bars. "Eventually . . ."

"So we wait. It'll be OK, right?" Niki asked as she sat down.

"It didn't look like Joseph was in God's plan," Jamal reminded her.

"But if he hadn't been sold as a slave, the whole world would've starved!" Chris said thoughtfully. "God's plan doesn't always make sense at first."

No sooner had he spoken than Niki gave a yelp. "The room's moving!" Simianne, who had been sitting on a pillow in the other part of the room, darted through the bars and landed on

Chris's neck. The cage descended into a dimly lit cavern. Below them light shimmered eerily on dark water. The cage came to rest on an island in the middle of a small underground lake. The door opened and the kids stepped out. Simianne clung to Chris, almost choking him.

"Cool!" Jamal said as the cage rose noiselessly back into the ceiling.

As the kids' eyes adjusted to the gloom they saw that the cavern's walls were covered in hieroglyphics. Statues and other artifacts were scattered around the cavern against the walls. "This is Egyptian stuff!" Niki exclaimed. "We're seeing what Joseph saw!" The kids excitedly pointed things out to each other.

After a while Jamal asked, "This is great, but how do we get out?"

"Well, everything's been in the Bible so far," Chris answered. "Let's read." He handed the Bible to Jamal.

Joseph

Joseph started out as his father's favorite. When he was a teenager his jealous brothers sold him as a slave. Talk about rejection! Through the experience he grew into a humble, God-dependent leader who became wise enough to save a nation! Joseph even forgave his brothers!

Verse: Genesis 50:20

"You planned to harm me. But God planned it for good. He planned to do what is now being done. He wanted to save many lives."

Moses, the Child

(Exodus 2)

In Egypt Israel's family grew into a nation. The Egyptians called them Hebrews and treated them well because of Joseph. Then, long after Joseph died, a new Pharaoh made them slaves. He ordered all baby Hebrew boys killed. He was afraid the Hebrews would become strong and rebel.

A Hebrew woman had a son. She saw that her baby was a fine child. So she hid him. When she couldn't hide him any longer, she got a basket and placed the child in it. She put the basket in the Nile River.

Pharaoh's daughter went to the Nile to take a bath. She saw the basket. When she opened it, she saw the baby. He was crying. She felt sorry for him.

She let the baby's mother look after him until he was older. Then he became her son. She named him Moses.

When Moses was grown up, he saw an Egyptian hitting a Hebrew man. Moses looked around and didn't see anyone. So he killed the Egyptian and hid his body in the sand.

When Pharaoh heard what had happened, he tried to kill Moses. But Moses escaped. He went to live in the desert.

Moses and the Burning Bush

(Exodus 3–4)

Forty years later, in the desert, the angel of the LORD appeared to Moses from inside a burning bush. The bush was on fire but didn't burn up.

God spoke to Moses from inside the bush. "Take off your sandals. The place you are standing on is holy ground." He continued, "I am the God of Abraham, Isaac and Jacob." When Moses heard that, he was afraid.

The LORD said, "I've seen my people suffer in Egypt. So I've come to save them from the Egyptians. I'll bring them out of that land into

a good land. I'm sending you to Pharaoh to bring the Israelites out of Egypt. They're my people."

God promised to go with Moses and told him what to say. He gave Moses miracles he could do to prove that he was telling the truth. One miracle changed his wooden staff into a snake! When Moses reached out and grabbed hold of the snake, it turned back into a staff.

God sent Moses' brother, Aaron, to help Moses.

Back in Egypt, Moses and Aaron gathered all the elders of Israel together. Aaron told them everything the LORD had said. He also did the miracles. They believed. They heard that the LORD was concerned about them. So they worshiped him.

"Even Moses made mistakes!" Niki exclaimed.

"Yeah, he was a murderer. But God chose him for his plan," Chris mused. "I wish I could figure out why."

"God chose him way before he killed the Egyptian or saw the burning bush or any of that stuff," Jamal said thoughtfully. "I mean, God saved him even when he was a baby!"

Niki nodded, "It seems like God had it all planned out."

"I'd love to see a bush like that, though," Jamal added. "Burning, burning but not burning. Hey, like a song!" He sang the words over and over again.

"Stop!" Chris laughed. "I wonder how God made it burn like that?"

"God can do anything!" Niki declared.

Jamal wandered toward the island's shore, trying to see across the water to the wall at the edge of the little lake. He could just make out a statue, some hieroglyphs and what might be a bush sitting among some boulders. Then he looked down. "Check this out!" he called. Chris and Niki rushed over. A basket of woven reeds was nestled against the shore.

"Hey, like Moses' basket!" Niki cried excitedly. "But, no baby–just a baby blanket. Maybe we have to put something into it."

"All we have is the Treasure Bible," Chris replied, "and we need that to figure out what to do."

"Look! The blanket has a picture of the Bible on it!" Jamal said. "I think we're supposed to put the Bible into the basket. Maybe we have to trust again like we've been learning," he suggested.

They looked at each other. Finally, Niki gingerly placed the Bible into the basket. As she let go, the Bible's weight triggered a hidden switch. The basket slid away from the shore and crossed the water to the opposite wall. A long wooden staff fell from the wall and landed with a plop on the basket. Near it the bush Jamal

---

Egyptian Archaeology

Why are Egyptian archaeologists always looking for mummies?

The main source of information on ancient Egypt is found in the huge tombs (pyramids) built by slaves for Egyptian kings (pharaohs). Pyramids were decorated with picture writing, called hieroglyphics. The Egyptians preserved their pharaohs' bodies as mummies and put them, with their possessions, into the tombs. The hieroglyphics, mummies and pyramids teach us a lot about Egypt.

Verse: Hebrews 11:24-25
"Moses had faith. So he refused to be called the son of Pharaoh's daughter. That happened after he had grown up. He chose to be treated badly together with the people of God. He chose that instead of enjoying sin's pleasures for a short time."

had glimpsed burst into flame! Simianne screeched and jumped. Then she clung to Jamal's shoulder. While Jamal comforted the monkey, the basket floated back to the island.

"That is great!" Jamal said as the bush burned, causing shadows to flicker across the room. "Now what?" Jamal lifted the Bible and staff out of the basket. "This is like Moses' staff or something," he said, hefting it. "Do we throw it down? Maybe it'll become a snake like in the story."

"No!" Niki yelled. "I hate snakes!" But the staff stayed a staff.

"Well, what else did Moses do with it?" Jamal asked.

"Maybe there's more. You read this time, Niki," Chris said.

The Plagues

(Exodus 7–11)

The LORD told Moses, "Pharaoh will refuse to listen to you. So I'll multiply my miracles in Egypt. Then the Egyptians will know that I am the LORD."

Moses asked Pharaoh to let the Israelites go. He refused. Through Moses God sent plagues. Using Moses' staff he turned water into blood. Then frogs covered the land. Later, dust became gnats.

Pharaoh's magicians said, "God has done this." But Pharaoh's heart was stubborn. He wouldn't listen.

God sent flies. Next, all the Egyptian livestock died. Then Moses threw ashes into the air and boils broke out on people and animals. Next was hail. It was the worst storm in Egypt's entire history.

God sent locusts to eat what was left.

But the LORD made Pharaoh's heart stubborn. He wouldn't let the people of Israel go. Then complete darkness covered Egypt for three days.

Pharaoh said to Moses, "Get out of my sight! Don't come to see me again! If you do, you'll die." Moses replied, "I'll never come to see you again."

Moses and Aaron did all those miracles. But the LORD made Pharaoh's heart stubborn. He wouldn't let the people of Israel go.

The Passover and Exodus

(Exodus 11–12)

The LORD said, "I'll bring one more plague. After that, Pharaoh will let you go. About midnight I'll go through every part of Egypt. Every oldest son in Egypt will die. I'll judge the gods of Egypt. I am the LORD."

Moses sent for the elders of Israel. He said, "Each family must kill a Passover lamb. Put some of the blood on the top and both sides of the doorframe. None of you go out of your house until morning. The LORD will go through the land to strike the Egyptians. He'll see the blood on the doorframes and pass over. He won't let the destroying angel kill you."

Moses told the people never to forget what God had done. The people worshiped God and did what Moses said.

At midnight the LORD struck down every oldest son in Egypt.

Pharaoh sent for Moses and Aaron. He said, "Get out of here! You and the Israelites! Go!"

The people of Israel lived in Egypt 430 years. At the end of 430 years all of the LORD's people marched out of Egypt like an army.

There were over 600,000 men plus women and children!

Crossing the Red Sea

(Exodus 14)

After the Israelites left, Pharaoh had second thoughts. Pharaoh and his officials said, "What have we done? We've lost our slaves and the work they used to do for us!"

The LORD made Pharaoh's heart stubborn. So he chased the Israelites. The people of Israel looked up. There were the Egyptians marching after them! They said to Moses, "Why did you bring us to the desert to die?" Moses answered, "Don't be afraid. You'll see how the LORD will save you."

The LORD said to Moses, "Hold your wooden staff out over the Red Sea to part the water." Moses reached out his hand. All night the LORD pushed the sea back with a strong east wind. The people of Israel went through the sea on dry ground. There were walls of water on their right and left. The Egyptians followed them.

The LORD said, "Reach out your hand. The waters will flow back over the Egyptians."

It happened just like God had said. Not one of the Egyptians was left. The LORD saved Israel from Egypt. So they put their trust in him.

They were on their way back to the land God had promised Abraham.

"Ugh, frogs and boils!" Niki shuddered.

"God was showing he could do whatever he said," Chris said thoughtfully. "He was showing the Egyptians he really was God."

"Hey! What if . . . ?" Jamal exclaimed, holding the staff over the water like Moses had. Nothing happened. "Oh, well. It was an idea."

"Look at this!" Chris called from the other side of the island. He pointed to a series of symbols chiseled into the rock. Next to each symbol was a hexagonal hole.

"They're pictures of the plagues!" Niki guessed. "Bring the staff." The end of the staff was hexagonal and looked just the right size.

"Wait!" Jamal yelled. "What if there's a certain order?"

"Good point," Chris agreed, holding the staff poised over a hole. "Read them out in order, Jamal." As Jamal read, Chris carefully put the staff into each hole. As he placed it into the last one they heard a loud THUMP!

"Whoa! Over here!" Niki called in awe. "Like the Red Sea parting!" The water, gurgling, was draining away from between two stone walls. The tops of the walls were just level with the water. They'd been invisible in the gloom.

"Awesome!" Jamal breathed.

"Think what the Israelites must have felt like when it really happened!" Chris said. "They'd sure have known God was real, huh?"

When the water was completely drained away, steps led down to the bottom of the lake and up the other side to a porch in front of three doorways.

"Which door?" Chris asked. "Let's think . . ." The mini-phone rang.

"Hi, kids," Dad said. "We're going to Madame Zamar's for supper. Be back in half an hour, OK?"

"Um, sure," Chris replied. He turned to the others after he hung up. "We gotta figure this out quickly. And hope we're close to the Globe Room."

"There!" Jamal pointed at stains on the top and sides of one of the

Moses

Moses had quite a life! Born a Hebrew slave, he lived 40 years as an Egyptian prince. Then he was a shepherd in the desert for 40 years. His last 40 years he led the whole nation of Israel from slavery to a new land. God called him "the most humble man on earth"!

Verse: Exodus 12:13
"The blood on your houses will be a sign for you. When I see the blood, I will pass over you. No deadly plague will touch you when I strike Egypt."

doors. "The Israelites were safe when they put blood on their doors, right? It's this one." He opened the door. Light poured down a stairwell toward them.

As they climbed, Niki asked, "Why'd God do that, with the blood and stuff?"

"We'll ask Mom and Dad," Chris said as they reached the top. They were back in the Globe Room! They had come out at the end of one of the short wings. A Pharaoh statue had slid aside to let them out.

The kids replaced the Bible and went outside. Simianne chattered good-by and disappeared. "Last one to the dig's a rotten egg!" Niki yelled and ran out of the castle.

"Oh yeah?" the boys called, racing after her.

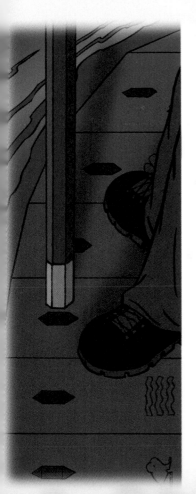

After cleaning up, the Delves and Jamal went to Madame Zamar's villa for supper. From her patio they had a wonderful view of the castle. It was good to relax in the cool evening air, enjoying the flowers and hearing the birds sing. When Zareef joined them they moved to the table. Zareef asked how the archaeological dig was going.

"We're still surveying the area," Dad answered. "But we've found some interesting pottery near the base of the cliff. We're concentrating our search there."

Mom turned to Madame Zamar, "This meal's wonderful! Is it local lamb?"

Madame nodded.

"Lamb?" Niki exclaimed. "We've been reading about lambs. Why did God tell the Israelites to kill lambs?"

"And put the blood on their doors?" Jamal asked. "That was weird!"

"The Passover's important, right?" Chris put in.

Mom chuckled. "You kids are sure fired up about the Bible."

"They must have found the old

Bible in the Castle," Zareef suggested. He turned to the kids. "The Passover is very important! A lamb was killed instead of the oldest son. God's angel saw the blood on the door and passed over the house. The death of a lamb instead of the death of a son."

Mom continued, "Do you remember we told you about God's plan? The Passover was God's promise to send another sacrifice, another 'lamb' that would save people for all time. With that first Passover God hinted at the heart of his plan for everyone."

"The Bible says there's no forgiveness without shedding blood," Dad added. "Remember that. It's important. God always does things for a reason. He used Noah to show that sin and wickedness must be judged. Through Abraham God taught that faith and trust are important. With Moses, God was teaching people who he is . . ."

"He's strong!" Niki interrupted. "He opened the Sea and everything!"

"Absolutely!" Mom agreed. "He protected and took care of his people.

He wanted them to know who he was. And he gave them the Law so they would know how he wanted them to live."

"The best way to live is in obedience to God," Madame Zamar put in. "God gave many rules about food, cleanliness, sacrifices, morals and all areas of life. He taught his people they couldn't make it on their own. They needed his help. The Law was important for that." She reached for a large, worn Bible. Before she began to read she showed the kids its gorgeous pictures. There was one of the Tabernacle, showing the ark of the covenant all covered in gold.

"Look at that!" Jamal exclaimed. "What is it?"

"I'll read you the story," Madame replied.

Passover

The Passover was the Great Feast of the Old Testament. It was first celebrated in Egypt when the angel of death "passed over" every household that had the blood of a lamb smeared on its doorframe. It was fulfilled when the blood of the Lamb of God, Jesus, was shed so that God would "pass over" our sins because of Jesus' death.

Verse: John 1:29
"Look! The Lamb of God! He takes away the sin of the world!"

The Ten Commandments and the Law

(Exodus 13, 19, 24, 31–32, 34)

From the Red Sea the LORD went ahead of the Israelites in a pillar of cloud. At night he led them with a pillar of fire. He led them to the mountain where Moses had seen the burning bush.

The LORD called to Moses. "Tell the Israelites, 'You've seen what I did to Egypt. Now obey me completely. Keep my covenant. If you do, you'll be my special treasure.'"

The LORD said to Moses, "Come up to me. I'll give you the stone tablets. They contain the Law and commands I've written to teach the people."

The glory of the LORD settled on Mount Sinai. The LORD wrote on the tablets the Ten Commandments. Then he gave Moses the tablets of the covenant written by the finger of God. Moses stayed on the mountain 40 days and 40 nights.

The people were impatient. So Aaron made them a god, a golden calf. They said, "Israel, here's your god who brought you up out of Egypt."

God knew what the people had done. He sent Moses back. Moses saw the calf. He burned with anger. He took the calf and burned it.

God punished the people for their sin.

The Tabernacle

(Exodus 25, 36, 40)

Later, God forgave the people. He gave other laws for all areas of life. Then the LORD said to Moses, "Tell the people to bring me an offering. Have them make a sacred tent for me. I'll live among them." He told Moses what they should bring and what to make.

Then Moses sent for every skilled worker to whom the LORD had given ability and who wanted to do the work. They received from Moses all the offerings the people had brought. The people kept bringing the offerings

they chose to give. So the skilled workers said to Moses, "The people are bringing more than enough for doing the work the LORD commanded us to do." So the people were kept from bringing more offerings.

When everything was ready, they set up the tent, called the Tent of Meeting or Tabernacle, in a large courtyard.

Then the cloud covered the Tent of Meeting. The glory of the LORD filled the holy tent. So the cloud of the LORD was above the holy tent during the day. Fire was in the cloud at night. The whole community of Israel could see the cloud during all of their travels.

"That picture of the Tabernacle was beautiful," Niki said back at camp as they got ready for bed. "The ark is where they kept the Ten Commandments, right?"

Dad nodded.

"Why did God give Moses the Ten Commandments?" Chris asked.

Mom answered, "Remember when Adam and Eve sinned and were sent away from God?" They all remembered that! "Well, God's big plan is to make a way for people to be with him–like before Adam and Eve disobeyed and were sent away."

"The Law's a big step in the plan," Dad continued. "God is holy.

Remember, sin separates us from God. So, for God to be with the Israelites, they needed to act in ways that weren't sinful or evil, ways that respected God and each other. The Ten Commandments told them how to do that."

Niki nodded and yawned.

"Bedtime," Mom said with a smile. "It's late."

The next morning Digger followed the kids back to the castle. They didn't notice him until he barked as they were crossing the courtyard. "Digger!" Niki exclaimed. "You want to come too?" She gave him a hug. "It's strange in here. You'll have to be careful!"

They retrieved the Bible and went through to the Globe Room. Digger ran around smelling everything!

"Hey look!" Jamal said, pointing to the globe. "The tablets! I didn't know what they were before." He rotated the globe until the tablet with a Roman numeral "I" matched a "I" on the floor. There was a soft click like a tumbler in a lock, then nothing.

"Another tablet!" Chris pointed. This one had the Roman numeral "II" on it. The kids matched it to its partner on the floor. Another quiet click. "It's like a combination lock," Chris said. They began to match all the tablets up to "X," ten in all.

After the last click a carving of a large pair of tablets on one wall slid apart. Behind it a flight of stairs led down to a small room. The room looked like the Tabernacle picture Madame Zamar had shown the kids. Torchlight sparkled on a gold-covered chest and flickered over cloths draped from the ceiling.

"Ooh! This is beautiful!" Niki breathed. "That must be like the ark!" The kids stared at everything in awe while Digger sniffed it all.

"Is this the treasure?" Jamal asked.

"It's what was in the Tabernacle," Chris said, doubtfully. "Maybe you'd better read, Niki. Let's find out what we do next." Niki opened the Bible and began where Madame Zamar had left off.

Ten Commandments

1. Don't worship any other god.
2. Don't make any idols.
3. Don't misuse God's name.
4. Keep the Sabbath day holy.
5. Honor your father and mother.
6. Don't murder.
7. Don't commit adultery.
8. Don't steal.
9. Don't give false witness.
10. Don't long for what belongs to others.

Verse: Deuteronomy 6:5
"Love the LORD your God with all your heart and with all your soul. Love him with all your strength."

The Twelve Spies

(Numbers 13–14)

The Israelites followed the cloud to the land God had promised to Abraham. Moses sent twelve spies to see what it was like. They found clusters of grapes so big two men had to carry them! After 40 days, the men returned. They gave Moses their report, "We went into the land you sent us to. It really does have plenty of milk and honey! But the people are powerful."

Caleb, one of the spies, interrupted. "We should go and take the land. We can certainly do it."

But the men who had gone with him spoke. "All the people we saw are very big and tall. We seemed like grasshoppers."

Joshua tore his clothes because he was angry. So did Caleb. They spoke to Israel. "We passed through the land and checked it out. It's very good. If the LORD is pleased with us, he'll give it to us."

But the people believed the bad report and were afraid.

The LORD was very angry because the people didn't trust him. God said that, of all those 20 and older, only Joshua and Caleb would enter the promised land. And, he said, the Israelites would wander 40 years in the desert before returning to take the land.

Joshua Leads Israel Across the Jordan

(Joshua 1, 3)

For 40 years the Israelites wandered in the desert as God had said. God looked after them. Then Moses blessed Joshua as the new leader.

When Moses died, God spoke to Joshua, "Joshua, I'll be with you, just as I was with Moses. Now then, I want you and all these people to get ready to go across the Jordan River.

"Speak to the priests who carry the ark of the covenant. Tell them, 'When you reach the edge of the Jordan, go into the water and stand there.'"

Joshua told the people, "The priests will carry the ark of the LORD. As soon as they step into the Jordan, it will stop flowing. The water coming down the river will pile up in one place."

The people prepared to go across. The priests carrying the ark of the covenant went ahead. The water of the Jordan was going over its banks. The priests' feet touched the water's edge. Right away the water coming down the river stopped flowing. The priests stood firm on dry ground in the middle of the river. They stayed there until the whole nation of Israel had gone across.

Jericho and the Victory Over Canaan

(Joshua 6, 10–11)

After crossing the Jordan, the Israelites came to the city of Jericho. The people of Jericho were afraid of Israel. They kept the city gates locked and guarded.

The LORD spoke to Joshua. He said, "I've handed Jericho over to you. March around the city once with all your fighting men. Do it for six days. Have seven priests carry trumpets made out of rams' horns. On the seventh day, march around the city seven times. Have the priests blow the

trumpets as you march. You'll hear them blow a long blast on the trumpets. When you do, order all of the men to give a loud shout. The walls of the city will fall down."

That's exactly what happened. When the walls fell down the army went straight in and took the city.

That was the first victory. God was fulfilling his promise to give the land to Abraham's descendants.

So Joshua brought the whole area under his control. He did it in one campaign. That's because the LORD, the God of Israel, fought for Israel. Joshua divided the land among the Israelites as their property. Then the land had peace.

"Cool!" Jamal exclaimed. "Rivers stopping, walls falling . . ."

"But how does that get us out of here?" Chris asked, looking around. Digger was sniffing at a tapestry on one wall, trying to get behind it. Woven into it with gold thread, the word "Promise" glistened. Chris eyed it. "Hmm. Promise," he mused. Then he cried, "The promise! God gave them the land he had promised to Abraham!"

Jamal jumped up and peered behind the tapestry. "There's a tunnel!" he announced.

"It looks small," Niki said doubtfully, peering over his shoulder.

"It's the only way out I can see," Chris told her. So they got on all fours and crawled down the tunnel one by one, Digger in the lead. It was a tight squeeze until the tunnel opened up and they could stand. Soon it became a steep, dark stairway winding downward. At the bottom Digger stopped dead and growled. Chris jerked to a stop so suddenly the others bumped into him. The dim room was full of huge warriors with weapons raised and threatening. A trick of the light made their stone eyes glint as if they were alive. They seemed to stare right at the kids.

Her eyes huge, Niki said, "Back we go." And she started to inch backward up the stairs.

"Wait!" Chris said. "We can't quit just because it's scary. That's what the Israelites did. There's no way I want to be stuck here 40 years or something, like they were!"

"Right. Let's be like Joshua and Caleb," Jamal suggested. "Let's go for it." They started cautiously across the room, keeping close together. Wherever they looked, huge warriors stared at them and threatened with weapons raised.

After what seemed forever, Niki whispered, "Listen! Water!" A happy gurgling sound led them to a river. On the other side was a large cavern.

"Phew!" Jamal breathed. "I can see why the Israelites were scared."

"God would have defeated the giants," Chris declared.

Joshua

Hey, did you know that Joshua is the only man in the Bible without parents? He was the son of "Nun"! Ha, ha! More seriously, Joshua was Moses' helper and learned leadership from him. He was also faithful, a warrior, a prayer, and, above all, a believer in God when others doubted.

Verse: Joshua 1:7
"Be strong and very brave. Make sure you obey the whole law my servant Moses gave you. Do not turn away from it to the right or the left. Then you will have success everywhere you go."

The only way across the river was by stepping-stones. Digger whined as he jumped from stone to stone, encouraged on by the kids. As the group crossed the cavern, their footsteps echoed hollowly. The far end was like a city wall made of stacked stones. Nearby, a ram's horn trumpet hung from a stalagmite.

"The priest's trumpet!" Niki shouted, reaching for it. As she tugged at the trumpet, there was a loud RUMBLE and the wall started to fall! Digger yelped. They all raced for the river.

Chris glanced back. The stones were falling slowly, forming a stairway! "Wait!" he called. "Look! Jericho with a difference! Come on!"

They ran forward again and started up the new stairs. "We better find out what's next, huh?" Niki suggested. So they sat on a step while Jamal read.

Deborah Leads Israel

(Judges 2, 4)

When Joshua and his generation died, those born after them grew up. They didn't know what the LORD had done for Israel. They deserted the LORD, the God of their people.

So God let their enemies defeat them. Israel suffered so much they cried for help. God gave them leaders to help defeat their enemies. But when the leaders died, the people returned to their evil ways. They followed other gods. The whole thing happened again and again.

One of those leaders was Deborah. People came to The Palm Tree of Deborah to see her. She told a warrior, Barak, that God said he should gather an army. God would help him defeat their enemy, Sisera. Barak agreed, but only if Deborah went too. He trusted in people more than God.

"All right," Deborah said. "But because of the way you're doing this, you won't receive any honor. The LORD will hand Sisera over to a woman.

"Go! Hasn't the LORD gone ahead of you?" As Barak's men marched out, the LORD drove Sisera away from the field of battle. Sisera's army was completely defeated. Sisera ran away. And, as Deborah had said, a woman killed him.

Samson

(Judges 13, 15–16)

There were other leaders after Deborah. One of them was Samson.

Once again Israel did what was evil in the sight of the LORD. So the LORD handed them over to the Philistines.

An angel told a woman, "You'll have a son. He mustn't cut his hair. He will be set apart to God from the day he's born. He'll begin to save Israel from the power of the Philistines."

God blessed the boy Samson.

One day, when Samson was grown, frightened Israelites tied him up. The Philistines came toward him shouting. The Spirit of the LORD came on Samson with power. The ropes became like burned thread. They dropped off. He found a fresh jawbone of a donkey. He grabbed it and struck down 1,000 men.

Later, Samson's girlfriend, Delilah, gave him to the Philistines. They cut his hair, making him weak. One day they had a huge party in their temple. They brought Samson in to mock him.

Samson prayed, "God, please make me strong just one more time." Samson reached toward the two pillars that held the temple up. He said, "Let me die with the Philistines!" Then he pushed with all his might.

The building collapsed! The Philistines were defeated!

95

When Jamal finished reading, Digger led the way up the stairs. The kids followed him to a plain circular room. Evenly spaced around the room were statues on pedestals. The walls behind and between the statues were covered with brightly colored murals. The kids split up to look at them. "This mural shows slaves!" Chris said. "Then the slaves look like they're praying. Then there's a big battle! Then another statue."

"This one's the same!" Jamal exclaimed.

"This too!" Niki added.

"Hmm, statue, mural showing slavery, prayer, fighting and victory, and the same all over again." Chris scratched his head. "Sounds like what we just read about the Israelites, huh? They kept getting conquered."

"These statues look . . . bad," Niki said, shuddering. "Like . . . hey! I wonder if they're idols!"

Jamal's stomach rumbled. "I'm starving! Let's eat," he suggested, rooting around in his backpack for food. Digger flopped down contentedly and wagged his tail, hoping for some lunch too.

Niki was still looking at the walls. "These guys prayed, then God sent people like Deborah and Samson. Maybe we should pray too."

"Good idea," Chris said. "Dear God, we're sure learning a lot about your book! This is an awesome place. But please help us understand. And thanks for the food. In Jesus' name, amen."

As they munched, the mini-phone rang. They all jumped, then crowded close to hear. "How's it going?" Dad asked.

Niki nudged Chris. "There's our answer to prayer!" she whispered, grinning.

"Great," Chris answered his dad, smiling. "Hey, in Judges, how come the Israelites kept getting conquered? Didn't God look after them?"

"Do you remember the Ten Commandments? The first commandment says to have no other gods or idols. Well, the Israelites started serving idols instead of God," Dad explained. "So God sent people to punish them and remind them they needed him. When they cried to God for help he sent leaders to rescue them. But they kept going back to the 'gods' of the nations around them."

"That was dumb!" Jamal commented.

"True. But sometimes we act like that too. Sometimes we let things or people become more important to us than God. That's the same as serving idols. God wants to be more important to us than anything."

Mom's voice came on the line. "Some people back then made right choices. Read Ruth."

"Thanks," the kids chorused as Chris hung up.

Jamal handed the Bible to Niki. "Your turn. Let's read."

Canaanite Idols.

Q: Which Canaanite idol had its own animal?

A: Baal, their chief god was often represented with or on a statue of a bull. The bull represented Baal's powers of fertility and strength. The Canaanites' other idols weren't movie or sports stars. They were carved female figures: Ashtoreth, who was Baal's wife, and Asherah, the goddess of the sea.

Verse: Mark 4:19

"But then the worries of this life come to them. Wealth comes with its false promises. The people also long for other things. All of those are the kinds of things that crowd out the message. They keep it from producing fruit."

Ruth

(Ruth 1, 3–4)

During a famine in the time of the judges, a family moved to another country. The man and his sons died. His wife, Naomi, returned to Israel. Ruth, her daughter-in-law, went with her. Ruth decided to follow God. She said, "Don't try to make me leave you. Where you go I'll go. Your people will be my people. Your God will be my God."

In those days a widow's closest relative was called a family protector. He protected the widow by marrying her.

Naomi's close relative, Boaz, liked Ruth. He cared for her and made sure she had food. One night Boaz said to Ruth, "Don't be afraid. There's a family protector more closely related to you than I am. If he wants to help you, good. But if he doesn't, then I'll do it."

In earlier times in Israel, there was a certain practice. One person would take his sandal off and give it to the other. That was how people in Israel showed that a business matter had been settled.

The family protector already had a family. So, to show he was willing to let Boaz take care of Ruth, he took his sandal off.

Then Boaz married Ruth. He cared for her and Naomi.

"Sandals!" Jamal laughed. "Something about this smells!"

"Weird, huh?" Chris chuckled. "The main thing is that Ruth chose to serve God. And it worked out great!"

Jamal jumped up. "Ruth served God instead of idols. Down with idols!" he yelled, grabbing a statue and pulling. To his surprise it fell forward on hinges. He grabbed another. The others joined in until all the idols were down. Digger raced around, barking at all the excitement.

"Look at this!" Chris said. The pedestal beneath the statue had an indent carved in it. "It's the shape of the Treasure Bible cover!"

"They all have it!" Jamal said, examining other pedestals. "Which one's the right one?"

"Maybe any?" Niki guessed. "You know, just choose God instead of an idol."

Chris fit the Bible cover into place on one of the empty pedestals. Immediately they heard a low rumbling. Part of a mural slid back and light poured through. "It's the Globe Room!" Niki cried as she darted through the opening. The boys ran after her. Digger followed, barking happily. They came out into one of the short wings. Several marble statues were spaced around the area. Suddenly they noticed Zareef, with Simianne on his shoulder, dusting a statue.

"Uh, hi!" Niki said in surprise. "We didn't know you knew about this place!"

Zareef smiled, moving farther into the room to dust another statue. "I am the caretaker. I must keep it clean and in good order, yes? It is beautiful, no? So many displays. They tell many, many stories. You have seen some, I think. From the Bible, yes? The creators of this were very interested in . . ." His voice trailed off mysteriously. The duster flicked Simianne's face. She squealed and jumped to Chris's shoulder.

Niki whispered to Chris, "Maybe he can help us figure things out."

Chris nodded and cleared his throat while he petted Simianne. "Um, we were wondering if you could help us. We've been trying to

Bible Kids

God loves kids! Samuel was called by God while he was still a boy. Joash and Josiah became kings when they were only 7 and 8 years old! David and Daniel began serving God as boys. Jeremiah was called to be a prophet while still "a youth." Even Isaiah probably became a prophet while a teenager!

Verse: Ruth 1:16
"But Ruth replied, 'Don't try to make me leave you and go back. Where you go I'll go. Where you stay I'll stay. Your people will be my people. Your God will be my God.'"

figure some things out with this Bible and . . ."

Zareef smiled and interrupted, "Good, good! You are enjoying yourselves. But children can do many things. You would be surprised. Like him," he pointed behind them to the first statue he'd been dusting. They all turned to look at it. It was the only kid-sized statue in sight.

"We . . . ," Niki began, turning back to Zareef. He was gone!

"How'd he do that?" Chris wondered aloud.

"He said kids can do stuff," Jamal reminded them. "We're kids! I guess it's up to us. I'll read!" He reached for the Bible.

Samuel

(1 Samuel 1, 3, 7)

Hannah couldn't have children. She promised that, if God gave her a son, he'd serve God all the days of his life. Soon after that she had a baby, Samuel. When he was still young, Hannah took Samuel to the priest, Eli, so he could live in the temple.

She said, "The LORD has given me what I asked him for. So now I'm giving this child to the LORD."

The boy Samuel served the LORD under the direction of Eli.

One night the LORD called out to Samuel. Samuel ran over to Eli. He said, "Here I am. You called out to me."

But Eli said, "I didn't call you. Go back and lie down." This happened three times. Then Eli told Samuel, "Go and lie down. If someone calls out to you again, say, 'Speak, LORD. I'm listening.'"

Samuel did as Eli said. God gave him a message. That was the beginning of Samuel's life as a judge and servant of God.

As Samuel grew up, the LORD was with him. Samuel spoke for God, and everything he said came true.

Samuel led Israel all the days of his life. He was Israel's last judge.

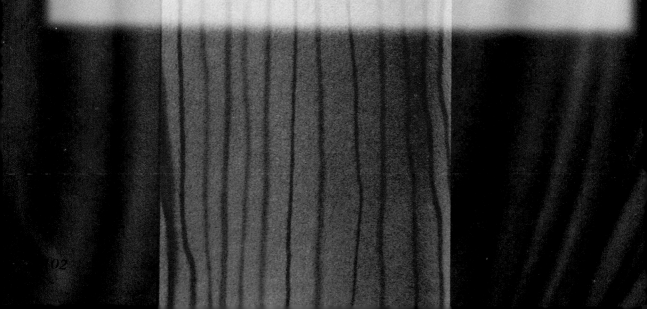

Saul

(1 Samuel 8, 10, 13)

When Samuel was old the people asked for a king. The LORD told Samuel, "I'm the one they don't want as their king. Let them have what they want. But give them a strong warning. Let them know what the king who rules over them will do."

So Samuel warned them a king would fight wars, take their land, and make their children serve him. They would become his slaves. But the people still wanted a king.

God chose Saul, the son of Kish, to be their king. But when it came time to make him king, they couldn't find him. The LORD said, "He has hidden himself among the supplies." So they ran over there and brought him out.

Then the people shouted, "May the king live a long time!"

Years later, Israel was at war. Samuel told Saul to wait for him. But Saul's men began to scatter. So Saul disobeyed and offered a sacrifice to God himself. Only priests were allowed to do that. Just as Saul finished, Samuel arrived. "What have you done?" he asked. "You did a foolish thing. You haven't obeyed the command God gave you. Now your kingdom won't last. The LORD has already looked for a man who is dear to his heart. He's appointed him leader of his people."

"Samuel obeyed God his whole life from when he was little!" Chris said. "God spoke to him as a kid!"

"God chose David young too!" Jamal added.

"I wonder if this is Samuel," Niki said, patting the statue of the boy. "Hey, look! He's holding . . . something. What is it?"

"It's a miniature menorah, a Hebrew candlestick," Chris declared, recognizing it. "But it has a hole in it. Weird! Hey!" he exclaimed suddenly. "Maybe it's a clue. Look! There's a hole in the statue's eye!" Chris moved around and put his head behind Samuel's. It was like

looking through Samuel's eye. Now he could see right through the menorah too. He was looking at a bookshelf near the corner. Centered in his view was a bright red book. "Niki, could you get that red book?" Chris asked eagerly. "Samuel here says it's important."

Excited, Niki dashed across the hall as Digger ran circles around her. "It's called *David and Goliath*," she said, tugging at the book. "It's stuck! Whoa!" With a loud THUNK the bookshelf jerked into motion! It pivoted into the wall taking Niki and Digger with it. Digger's whining faded into silence as the movement

stopped. Simianne squealed and hid behind the Samuel statue.

"Niki!" Chris shouted. He ran to where the bookshelf had been. But the wall was closed tight. "We better figure out how to find her," he told Jamal, concerned. "We have the Treasure Bible. She won't be able to figure stuff out without it!"

"Look at this, Chris," Jamal said. "Samuel here moved when the bookshelf did. Now his key thing is pointing at that blue book on the other bookshelf!"

"Maybe it'll help us find Niki," Chris suggested. "Come on. We're sticking together this time." Jamal and Simianne joined Chris by the bookshelf. Chris tried to remove the blue book, titled *David*

and Jonathan's Friendship. The bookshelf swung around like they had hoped and deposited them in an empty, dimly lit hallway. They followed the hallway to some stairs. The stairs led to a room. But no Niki.

Meanwhile, trying to trigger the bookshelf to turn back to the Globe Room, Niki jiggled the book. It came out in her hands. "Now what?" she asked the dog. "Boy! I'm glad you're with me, Digger." She gave him a big hug, then rose and looked around. She was in a room full of armor, spears, swords, ropes and knives. It smelled of metal and old leather. "Look at this stuff!" she breathed in amazement. "The guys would love it!" Digger barked agreement, then sniffed at the book in her hands. "Good idea, Digger. Let's read." Niki read her book to Digger unaware that nearby the boys had decided to read from the Treasure Bible.

Israel's Neighbors

Q: What do the Philistines, Amorites, Hittites, Perizzites and Jebusites have in common?

A: They were all bad neighbors to the Israelites. The warlike Philistines were always fighting with them. The Amorites were probably the worst neighbors though, because they led the Israelites away from God.

Verse: 1 Samuel 15:23

"Refusing to obey him is as sinful as using evil magic. Being proud is as evil as worshiping statues of gods. You have refused to do what the Lord told you to do. So he has refused to have you as king."

David and Goliath

(1 Samuel 17)

While Saul was still king, he fought the Philistines. A soldier over nine feet tall, Goliath, kept shouting for someone to fight him. David trusted God. He knew he could beat Goliath with God's help, so he stepped forward. Saul offered him armor. But David wasn't used to it. So he didn't wear it.

Goliath saw how young David was. He hated him. He said to David, "Why are you coming at me with sticks? Do you think I'm only a dog? Come over here."

David said, "You're coming to fight against me with a sword, a spear and a javelin. But I'm coming against you in the name of the LORD who rules over all. This very day the LORD will hand you over to me. Then the whole world will know there's a God in Israel."

As Goliath moved closer to attack him, David ran quickly to meet him. He took out a stone. He put it into his sling. He slung it at Goliath. The stone hit him on the forehead and sank into it.

The Philistines saw that their hero was dead. So they ran away.

After that, David became very popular. The people loved him.

But Saul became jealous of him.

David and Jonathan

(1 Samuel 18, 20, 23)

Jonathan was Saul's son. He and David became close friends.

Jonathan made a covenant with David because he loved him just as he loved himself. He took off the robe he was wearing and gave it to David. He even gave him his sword, his bow and his belt.

One day Saul threw a spear at David. David asked Jonathan to find out if Saul wanted to kill him. They arranged a signal. David would hide in a field. If Saul wanted to kill David, Jonathan would shoot his arrows far out into the field. If Jonathan shot only a little way into the field, David was safe.

The next morning Jonathan shot arrows far into the field. David came out of hiding. The two friends were very sad.

Jonathan said, "Go in peace. In the name of the LORD we've taken an oath. We've promised to be friends. We've said, 'The LORD is a witness between you and me, between your children and my children forever.'"

Jonathan told David that God would make him strong. "Don't be afraid," he said. "My father Saul won't lay a hand on you. You'll be king over Israel."

"David and Jonathan were friends like us," Jamal declared when they'd read the story.

Chris agreed. "They would've died for each other! That's friendship!" He frowned. "We have to find Niki, Jamal. What if she's stuck or something?"

"Don't sweat it. We'll work together like David and Jonathan did. We'll find her."

"Yeah, God has a plan, right?" Chris agreed. "Whoever made this place had a plan too. We'll just trust God like we've been learning to do." Chris surveyed the room. "How do we get out?" Wall paintings showed David and Jonathan hunting, praying, talking . . . just being friends. The boys had forgotten about Simianne until she chattered at them from an opening high on one wall.

Jamal pointed to the monkey. "Maybe that's the way out."

"We're too short to reach it," Chris protested, eyeing the distance.

"Not if we work together. Climb on my shoulders!"

Chris scrambled onto Jamal's shoulders and peered into the opening. "I hear Digger!" he exclaimed. "I'll be right back." He pulled himself up, crawled after Simianne to the end of the narrow tunnel and peered out. He was looking down at Digger and Niki! The dog whined happily.

"What is it, Digger?" Niki asked. Simianne dropped onto her shoulder. Niki yelped. She glanced up to see where the monkey had come from and saw Chris's grinning face. "Chris! Am I glad to see you!" she exclaimed in relief.

"We knew we'd find you!" Chris declared. "Hey, toss me that rope. I'll go get Jamal." Niki threw Chris a rope from the wall. He tied it around himself, crawled back to Jamal and lowered the other end to his friend. Jamal scrambled up. Soon they were all together in the weapons room.

"What now?" Jamal asked.

"We-ell," Niki said, "David used a sling . . ." She retrieved a sling from among the other weapons. A stone was nestled in its leather pouch.

Friendship in the Bible

Ecclesiastes says, "Two are better than one." Everyone needs a buddy! Choosing the right friend is important. Elijah took Elisha from his farm and showed him how to be an obedient prophet. Barnabas helped Paul get started in his ministry. Priscilla and her husband, Aquila, taught together. Even Jesus had a special friend, John, "the disciple Jesus loved."

Verse: Proverbs 17:17
"Friends love at all times. They are there to help when trouble comes."

Chris pointed at a huge statue with a dent in its forehead. "That must be Goliath. Maybe we have to get the stone in the dent. Like David."

"Lift me up," Niki suggested, "I'll push the stone in." As the stone filled the dent the statue CREAKED ponderously aside. The kids followed the narrow passage behind it to a circular room. Twelve evenly spaced doors were labeled with Jacob's sons' names.

"We've been here before!" Jamal announced. "Last time we used the 'Joseph' door!" He yanked that door open. "Hey! Where did the room go?"

"There's no door with 'David' on it, either," Chris stated. "We better read!"

David Becomes King

(1 Samuel 16; 2 Samuel 9)

After Saul disobeyed God, God sent Samuel to Bethlehem to anoint a new king from among the sons of Jesse (Ruth's grandson), from the tribe of Judah.

Samuel saw Jesse's oldest son. The LORD said to Samuel, "Don't consider how handsome or tall he is. I don't look at the things people look at. I look at what's in the heart." Then Jesse's youngest son David came in. The LORD said, "Get up and anoint him. He's the one." So Samuel anointed David in front of his brothers.

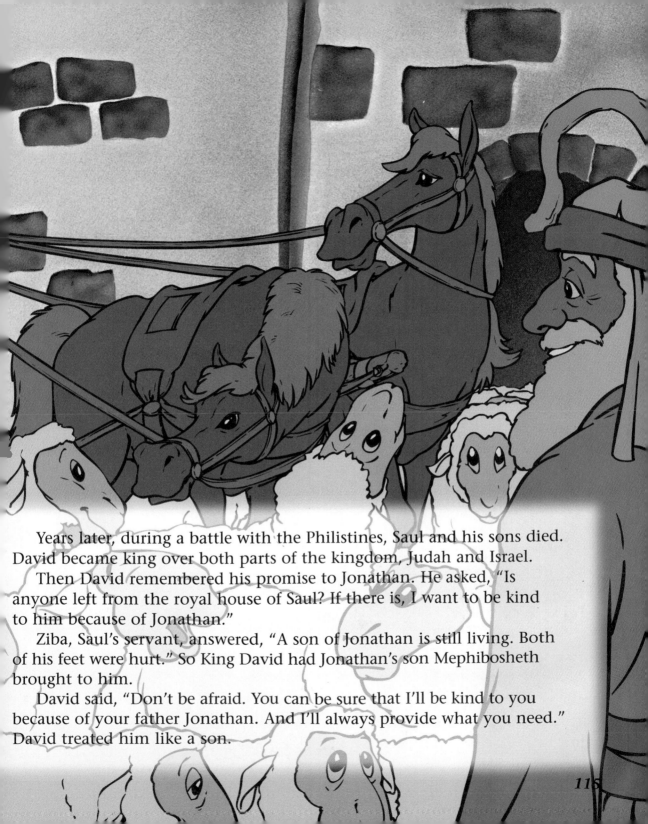

Years later, during a battle with the Philistines, Saul and his sons died. David became king over both parts of the kingdom, Judah and Israel.

Then David remembered his promise to Jonathan. He asked, "Is anyone left from the royal house of Saul? If there is, I want to be kind to him because of Jonathan."

Ziba, Saul's servant, answered, "A son of Jonathan is still living. Both of his feet were hurt." So King David had Jonathan's son Mephibosheth brought to him.

David said, "Don't be afraid. You can be sure that I'll be kind to you because of your father Jonathan. And I'll always provide what you need." David treated him like a son.

"It sounds like David sure took God's promises seriously!" Jamal said.

"But how does that tell us which door to take?" Niki wondered.

"Hmm. David . . . Jesse . . . Ruth," Chris murmured. Suddenly, startling everyone, he shouted, "Judah!" Simianne dove behind Jamal then, with her head safely tucked between Jamal's elbow and side, she scolded Chris. "David was from the tribe of Judah!" Chris explained as he pulled the 'Judah' door open. Stairs led downward. "All right! The answer was right in the Bible as usual!" Digger was first through the door.

As they descended, the kids heard water falling and faint music. The stairs opened into a gorgeous room full of light and music. A soft breeze brushed their faces. Brightly colored tapestries, paintings and statues filled the room. To one side a large throne stood, covered with gold and precious stones. A waterfall flowed down one wall into a basin. Its

splashing turned a wheel that played quiet music. Wind-chimes moved gently. The fragrance of roses filled the air.

"This is beautiful!" Niki breathed. "Peaceful. Like a garden . . ."

The kids wandered around looking at everything, speaking reverently. "That must be Goliath's sword," Chris whispered, pointing to a huge, black iron sword mounted on the wall.

"Check out this throne!" Jamal said, sitting on it. "Could this be the treasure we're looking for?"

"Hmm, what about the plan?" Chris wondered. "We're supposed to follow it to the treasure. I don't think this is it, Jamal."

"Here's David's harp," Niki interrupted. "He was a singer, right? I wonder if this is David's room. All this stuff is about him."

One wall held a set of large scrolls, half unrolled. Jamal turned the handle beneath them. The parchment rolled from one scroll to the other. "What's it say?" Jamal asked, busily turning.

"These are psalms!" Chris declared, looking over Jamal's shoulder. "David wrote lots of psalms. Remember, Niki?"

"Yeah." Niki turned to Jamal, proud that she could explain. "Psalms are worship songs. They're about how great God is. They tell him we love him and want to serve him and stuff. David wrote them for God and sang them in the temple. Right, Chris?"

"Right! Others wrote psalms too. But David wrote the most."

"Let's sit by the waterfall and read some!" Niki suggested. She leaned against the fall's basin and watched the light filter through a skylight, reflect off the water and shimmer across the walls and tapestries. The boys sprawled on the ground nearby. Simianne groomed Digger as Jamal read.

David

David was a leader from the start! He fought giants and lions as a teenager. He became a great king who was a man after God's own heart.

He used his musical skills and love for God to write many of the psalms we still sing today.

Verse: I Samuel 16:7
"I do not look at the things people look at. They look at how someone appears on the outside. But I look at what is in the heart."

Introduction to Psalms

(Psalm 1)

David and others wrote of their love for God in poems and songs called psalms. Some psalms focus on God and his actions. Some are used for group praise and worship and tell God about people's love and commitment. Some psalms thank God for who he is and what he does. Others just tell God how we feel–happy, sad, worried or confused.

Psalm 1 says people living God's way are blessed. God watches over them.

Psalm 1

Blessed are those who obey the law
of the Lord.
They don't follow the advice
of evil people.
They don't make a habit of doing
what sinners do.
They don't join those who make
fun of the Lord and his law.
Instead, they take delight in the law
of the Lord.
They think about his law day and
night.
They are like a tree that is planted
near a stream of water.
It always bears its fruit at the
right time.
Its leaves don't dry up.
Everything godly people do turns
out well.
The Lord watches over the lives of
those who are godly.
But the lives of sinful people will
lead to their death.

A Praise Psalm

(Psalm 150)

Psalm 150 is a celebration song. It's like a party where everyone shouts out how good God is, making music with anything they can get their hands on.

Psalm 150

Praise the LORD.

Praise God in his holy temple.
    Praise him in his mighty heavens.

Praise him for his powerful acts.
    Praise him because he is greater
        than anything else.

Praise him by blowing trumpets.
    Praise him with harps and lyres.

Praise him with tambourines and
        dancing.
    Praise him with stringed
        instruments and flutes.

Praise him with clashing cymbals.
    Praise him with clanging cymbals.

Let everything that has breath praise
        the LORD.

Praise the LORD.

The Shepherd's Psalm

(Psalm 23)

David knew that God loves and takes care of his people. In Psalm 23 David tells how God guides us and protects us through whatever happens in life.

Psalm 23

The L ORD is my shepherd. He gives
   me everything I need.
   He lets me lie down in fields of
    green grass.
He leads me beside quiet waters.
   He gives me new strength.
He guides me in the right paths
   for the honor of his name.
Even though I walk
   through the darkest valley,
I will not be afraid.
   You are with me.
Your shepherd's rod and staff
   comfort me.
You prepare a feast for me
   right in front of my enemies.
You pour oil on my head.
   My cup runs over.
I am sure that your goodness and love
   will follow me
   all the days of my life.
And I will live in the house of the
   L ORD
   forever.

"Psalm 23 is my favorite," Niki said sleepily. The quiet music and waterfall splashing in the background were like a soft lullaby. Everything was peaceful until Simianne pounced on Digger's tail. He yelped and leaped to his feet, growling. Simianne fled across the room screeching, with Digger in pursuit. The kids laughed at their antics. The animals chased each other around the room. Then they disappeared. "Where did they go?" Niki wondered.

"Behind the waterfall," Chris answered. "What are they doing?"

"They found something!" Jamal cried as he jumped up to look. There was a narrow path behind the fall. Jamal followed it. His voice came floating back like an echo. "Cool! A cave!"

Chris and Niki scrambled up and followed. Water splashed into a small cave behind the waterfall. Walking through the cave was like moving through a thick mist. Past the waterfall the cave became a tunnel, then a narrow stairway winding upward. The stairs ended at a heavy cloth. When the kids peered past it, they discovered they were behind a tapestry in the Globe Room.

"What now?" Jamal asked as they squeezed past the tapestry. They were in the long wing. "Do we find a clue about the psalms? What time is it?"

"Feels like supper time," Chris said, glancing at his watch. "It is. Let's go." They exited the Globe Room and put the Bible back so the outside door would open. Simianne left them at the gate as they headed down the hill.

When the kids reached the camp their parents were excited. They had found part of a stone tablet with map-like markings etched into it. "I just know this is it!" Mom told them enthusiastically. "When we find

Psalm Reference Guide.

Psalms can take you to God even when you're struggling.

When you:
- Need courage
  Read: Psalm 23 and 27
- Need faith
  Read: Psalm 46
- Need physical strength
  Read: Psalm 91
- Need forgiveness
  Read: Psalm 51
- Need comfort and protection
  Read: Psalm 121
- Need help to do right
  Read: Psalm 1 and 73
- Need encouragement and hope
  Read: Psalm 40 and 139
- Want to thank God
  Read: Psalm 8, 100 and 103

Verse: Ephesians 5:19-20
"Speak to each other with psalms, hymns and spiritual songs. Sing and make music in your heart to the Lord. Always give thanks to God the Father for everything. Give thanks to him in the name of our Lord Jesus Christ."

the other piece it'll lead us right to Tresor's Caverns!"

Over supper, the parents talked about their progress at the dig. Later, the kids asked about the psalms. "Some psalms were prophetic," Dad explained. "That means they talked about things that would happen hundreds of years later. And," he added with a grin, "psalms are meant to be sung. How about singing some?"

The kids agreed eagerly. They helped Dad build up the fire while Mom got out her guitar. Between singing psalms and campfire songs they roasted marshmallows. Digger joined enthusiastically in the singing.

"David really loved God," Niki commented later. "He was the greatest Israelite king, right?"

Mom nodded. "He followed God with all his heart. But his son, Solomon, was great too . . . in a different way. Why don't we read about him?" She got out the Bible and started to read.

Solomon, His Wisdom and Wealth

(1 Kings 2–4)

David ruled Israel for many years. His family was important to God's plan. When he was old he told his son Solomon, "Do everything the LORD your God requires. The LORD will keep the promise he made to me. 'Your sons must be faithful to me with all their heart and soul. Then you'll always have a man sitting on the throne of Israel.'"

After Solomon became king God spoke to him in a dream. "Ask for anything you want."

Solomon answered, "LORD my God, you've put me in the place of my father David. But I'm only a little child. I don't know how to carry out my duties. So give me a heart that understands. Then I can tell the difference between what's right and what's wrong."

The LORD was pleased. So God said to him, "Because that's what you've asked for, I'll give it to you. And that's not all. I'll give you riches and honor. As long as you live, no other king will be as great as you are. Obey my laws and commands, just as your father David did."

God made Solomon very wise. The kings of all of the world's nations heard how wise Solomon was. So they sent their people to listen to him.

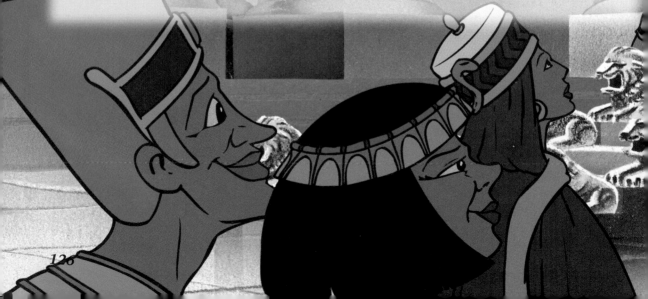

127

Solomon Builds the Temple

(2 Chronicles 3, 5–7)

All this time the Israelites still came to the Tabernacle, the tent they'd made in the desert, to meet with God. When Solomon was king, he built a beautiful, permanent temple for God in Jerusalem, the capital city. He covered the inside of the temple with pure gold. He decorated it with valuable jewels.

Aaron's descendants served God in the Tabernacle as priests. When the temple was finished they put the ark of God's covenant inside the temple and celebrated.

Solomon brought sacrifices. The trumpet players and singers made music together. They sang, "He is good. His faithful love continues forever."

Solomon said, "Lord, you're the God of Israel. There's no God like you in heaven or on earth. You keep the covenant you made with us. You show us your love when we follow you with all our hearts. But will you really live on earth with human beings? After all, even the highest heavens can't hold you. My God, let your ears pay attention to the prayers offered in this place." Solomon finished praying. Then fire came down from heaven. It burned up the burnt offering and the sacrifices.

God's presence filled the temple.

Proverbs

(Proverbs 1, 2, 10, 12, 17)

Solomon wrote many wise sayings, called proverbs, to teach people the best way to live. He said:

"Be wise: If you really want to gain knowledge, you must begin by having respect for the LORD. A wise heart accepts commands. Call out for the ability to be wise. Look for it as you would look for silver. Search for it as you would search for hidden treasure.

"Work hard and listen to advice: Hands that work hard will rule. But

people who don't want to work will become slaves. The ways of foolish people seem right to them. But wise people listen to advice.

"Be careful what you say: Thoughtless words cut like a sword. But the tongue of wise people brings healing. The LORD hates those whose lips tell lies. But he's pleased with people who tell the truth.

"Be a good friend: Those who erase a sin by forgiving it show love. But those who talk about it come between close friends. Friends love at all times. They are there to help when trouble comes."

Unfortunately, Solomon didn't always act wisely. He married many women from nations that served other gods. He started to follow their evil ways and stopped obeying God's Law.

In the morning the kids explored the Globe Room for clues about what they'd read the night before. "Check this out!" Jamal called, pointing to a row of marble pillars in one of the short side wings. "They're huge! Did Solomon's temple have these?"

Chris peered between two pillars. An archway led to a long room. "Zareef! Hi!" Chris called. Zareef was sitting at a high desk studying old parchments. He waved the kids in.

Simianne dropped onto Niki's shoulder as she entered. Niki laughed and tickled the monkey behind her ear, "Wondered where you were this morning." The room was lined with bookshelves containing books, neatly racked scrolls, and pottery. Models of towns and buildings rested on tables in the center of the room. The boys wandered around while Zareef continued reading. Niki curled up on a cushion with Simianne and leafed ahead in the Treasure Bible.

Chris called across the room to Zareef, "Is this Solomon's room?"

"Yes, yes," Zareef answered, rolling up his parchment. "His wisdom room. Solomon learned that true wisdom comes only by knowing God. Wisdom teaches us how to live successfully–by obeying God's laws, working hard and being honest."

"Solomon was really wise, wasn't he?" Jamal asked.

"No one was like Solomon!" Zareef agreed. "While he was a young man, he followed his own advice to search for wisdom as if searching for hidden treasure."

The boys exchanged looks and grinned at each other. "Hidden treasure!" Chris whispered. "We're close!" When they looked around, Zareef was gone.

Jamal shook his head in wonder. "How does he keep doing that? Well, let's search! The treasure's close, Niki!"

Niki closed the Bible and eagerly joined the boys. Examining models of buildings and cities she suggested, "This must be what Solomon built!"

"You're right! The temple should be here," Chris guessed, coming over. "It was covered in gold!"

"Ooh!" Niki breathed. "This one! It's gorgeous!" Niki tried to lift the model to look at it more closely, but it was hinged to the table. As it tilted, a bookshelf rumbled outward. Simianne wrapped her tail around Niki's neck and held on tightly.

"Come on!" Jamal yelled, running toward the bookshelf. The kids stumbled through the opening and down some stairs into a long rectangular room lit by high, narrow windows. The floor was covered with a large map. "Whoa!" Jamal said, walking across it. "What's this?"

"I recognize it!" Chris exclaimed. "It's the Kingdom of Israel. Maybe while Solomon was king? Let's read!"

Solomon's Books

Solomon left us his wisdom in the book of *Proverbs*. Many people also believe he wrote two more wise books. *Song of Songs* tells of the beauty and wonder of married love. *Ecclesiastes*, probably written by Solomon when he was very old, tells how meaningless life is without God.

Verse: Proverbs 1:7
"If you really want to gain knowledge, you must begin by having respect for the LORD. But foolish people hate wisdom and training."

The Nation Splits

(1 Kings 11–12)

Near the end of his life, Solomon forgot his own advice. He worshiped his wives' gods. God was very disappointed. He said he'd tear the kingdom away from Solomon's son. He said, "But I'll give him one of the tribes because of my servant David."

Solomon's son Rehoboam became the next king. Jeroboam, one of Solomon's officials, and the whole community of Israel went to Rehoboam. They said, "Your father put a heavy load on our shoulders. But now make our hard work easier. Then we'll serve you."

The elders agreed with them. But the king didn't accept the advice the elders had given him. Instead, he followed the advice of the young men. He said, "My father put a heavy load on your shoulders. But I'll make it even heavier." So the king didn't listen to the people. That's because the LORD had planned it that way.

All of the people of Israel saw that the king refused to listen to them. They said, "We don't have any share in David's royal family. Take care of your own kingdom!" Israel made Jeroboam their king.

Only the tribe of Judah stayed with David's family, as God said. So the kingdom was divided in two, Israel and Judah.

"Solomon wrecked the whole kingdom by worshiping those other gods!" Jamal exclaimed in disgust.

"That's what happens when you forget God," Chris agreed. "Even the wisest person can blow it!" He wandered across the map. "This must be Israel before Rehoboam became king," he muttered. "I wonder where the kingdoms separated."

Jamal found a large, long-handled wooden wheel set into the stone to one side of the map. The wheel was parallel to the floor. "Cool!" Jamal exclaimed, walking around it. "Help me, Niki." The two threw their weight against the handles until the wheel turned, squeaking protest. There was a deep grating sound and the map began to split in two! "Look out, Chris!" Jamal called.

Chris was straddling the widening split. He threw himself to one side just in time, laughing. "That's my answer. The kingdom split right there!"

When the wheel was fully turned, the floor had split wide open. Two stairways descended into the split from opposite sides. At the foot of each was a solid wooden door. One door was marked "Israel," the other "Judah."

"Rehoboam should've listened to Israel," Niki declared. "They were the good guys! We should search for the treasure behind the Israel door!" She ran down the stairs.

"Wait, Niki," Chris called after her. "We should try the Judah door because of David. God saved Judah for David's family."

"Well, *I* think the treasure will be in Israel," Niki said stubbornly, holding her arm up to Simianne. The monkey jumped to Niki's shoulder as Niki yelled, "I'll beat you to it!" She yanked the door open and disappeared into the darkness beyond.

"Come on!" Chris called to Jamal, "We'll find it first. This way!" The boys ran down the other stairway and flung open the door marked "Judah."

Before Niki could change her mind the door whooshed shut behind her and fire leaped up right in front of her! She jumped back in surprise. Just inside the door, flames licked across a sacrifice burning on a large altar. In the flickering light she saw that the walls near the altar were covered with mosaics of men dancing and shouting. Niki wondered if she'd chosen the wrong door after all.

At the far end of the long room, visible in the shifting light from the fire, Niki could just make out an opening surrounded by what looked like sharp teeth. "Hey, I think I know what this is," she told Simianne hopefully. "I read ahead in the Bible upstairs." And Niki began to tell Simianne the stories.

Archaeology/History of Jerusalem

Jerusalem is almost 5000 years old–just imagine! It's been destroyed and rebuilt so many times that, in places, the rubble of the ruins under some of the houses is almost seventy feet deep! The whole city of Jerusalem has been rebuilt on the same spot at least five times!

Verse: 1 Samuel 15:22
"But Samuel replied, 'What pleases the LORD more? Burnt offerings and sacrifices, or obeying him? It is better to obey than to offer a sacrifice. It is better to do what he says than to offer the fat of rams.'"

Elijah, Prophet to Israel

(1 Kings 18)

King Jeroboam and the Israelite kings after him served other gods like Baal. God sent messengers, called prophets, to call the people back to him. The prophet Elijah challenged Israel and Baal's followers. "If the LORD is the one and only God, follow him. But if Baal is the one and only God, follow him."

Elijah and Baal's prophets prepared bulls for sacrifice. Elijah said, "You pray to your god. And I'll pray to the LORD. The god who answers by sending fire down is the one and only God."

Baal's prophets prayed all day.

"Shout louder!" Elijah said. "Perhaps Baal has too much to think about. Or maybe he's gone to the toilet." So they shouted louder. No one answered.

Elijah poured twelve barrels of water over his altar. He prayed, "Today let everyone know that you're God in Israel. LORD, answer me. Then these people will know that you're the one and only God. They'll know that you're turning their hearts back to you again."

The fire of the LORD came down. It burned up the sacrifice, the wood, the stones and the soil. It even licked up the water in the ditch! All of the people saw it. They cried out, "The LORD is the one and only God!"

Jonah and the Whale

(Jonah 1–3)

God cared about other nations too. He sent a prophet, Jonah, to preach to the city of Nineveh.

Nineveh was Israel's enemy so Jonah didn't want to go. He ran away on a ship. But the LORD sent a strong wind over the Mediterranean Sea. A wild storm came up. It was so wild that the ship was in danger of breaking apart.

The sailors found out Jonah was running away from the LORD. They became terrified. They asked Jonah, "What should we do to make the sea calm down?"

"Pick me up and throw me into the sea," he replied. "Then it will become calm. I know it's my fault that this terrible storm has come on you." Then they took Jonah and threw him overboard. And the stormy sea became calm.

But the LORD sent a huge fish to swallow Jonah. Jonah was inside the fish for three days and three nights. From inside the fish Jonah prayed to the LORD his God. The LORD gave the fish a command. It spit Jonah up onto dry land.

Then Jonah preached to Nineveh. He announced, "In 40 days Nineveh will be destroyed." The people of Nineveh believed God's warning. God saw that they stopped doing what was evil. So he took pity on them. He didn't destroy them as he had said he would.

Israel's Rebellion

(2 Kings 17)

Nineveh repented, but Israel didn't. God wanted his people to follow him from their hearts, not just with words. But after telling Elijah they would follow God, Israel kept turning away. God warned them they would be conquered and taken away from the land because of their sin.

The LORD warned Israel through all of his prophets and seers. He said, "Turn from your evil ways. Keep my commands and rules. Obey every part of my Law." But the people wouldn't listen. They didn't trust in the LORD their God. They refused to obey his rules. They broke the covenant he had made with them. They didn't pay any attention to the warnings. They worshiped worthless statues of gods. They followed the example of the nations that were around them. They did the very things the LORD had told them not to do. So the LORD turned his back on all of the people of Israel.

God's warnings came true when the king of Assyria marched into the land of Israel. He took the people of Israel away from their own land. He sent them off to Assyria. All this took place because the people of Israel had committed sins against the LORD their God. They worshiped other gods.

"Nineveh was Israel's enemy," Niki told Simianne. "It was the capital of Assyria. No wonder Jonah didn't want to go there! But God loves everyone! Nineveh and Assyria too." She strolled down the room. "Look," she said, pointing to mosaics on the wall. "This must be Israel being taken away by Assyria."

Niki came to the far end of the room with its strange tooth-ringed opening. "Maybe this is supposed to be the big fish's mouth. Anyway, it looks like the only way out." Niki stepped over the teeth into a room whose walls were rib-shaped and covered with pictures of sea life. She sighed. "I really blew it! No Bible, no boys. No treasure either, huh?" Simianne murmured comfortingly in her ear.

Niki ran her hands over the ribbed walls. "What did Zareef say?" she wondered. "'Search for wisdom as for treasure.' Ohh!" she breathed. She whacked herself on the forehead

ightly. "What a silly I am. The treasure Solomon meant was wisdom! Not gold and stuff! I wasn't very wise, huh?"

Simianne leaped from Niki's shoulder to the floor and began to groom her belly. Head bent, intent on her work, she looked like someone praying.

Niki smiled. "Thanks, Simianne. That's a good idea. If I'm trapped like Jonah, I should do what he did, right? He prayed. God forgave him and helped him when he asked. It was the same with the Ninevites too. They prayed and God spared them." Niki sat on the floor next to Simianne and prayed. "Dear God, I was looking for the wrong treasure. Chris is good at figuring things out, but I wanted to show him I was too. Please forgive me for not doing things your way. Help me to be wise and figure out how to get out of here. In Jesus' name, amen."

Niki opened her eyes and looked around. The backs of the teeth at the entrance caught her eye. They were engraved with pictures and letters. She knelt to see better in the flickering firelight. "These don't make sense, Simianne." Niki said slowly. "Hmm. What if . . . that's it!" she shouted. "These letters would spell 'obey' if they were in a different order! Jonah finally obeyed. I want to too." She tried to rearrange the stone teeth. They didn't move. But they THUNKED as Niki pressed them in order, spelling 'obey.' The entrance closed slowly like huge jaws. The room rumbled and shook. It felt like it was turning. Simianne cowered against Niki's chest. The shaking stopped. Slowly the jaws opened again. She was facing a brightly lit, colorful room.

"Thank you, God!" Niki cried, stepping out and happily swinging Simianne around in a circle. "All right!"

Swallowed Whole

Did you know? In 1891 James Bartley, a harpooner, disappeared while hunting a large sperm whale. A day and a half later his buddies found James inside the whale's stomach! He was unconscious from fright but unharmed. In fact, the whale shark, white shark and sperm whale can all probably swallow a man whole. Talk about a mouthful!

Verse: Psalm 51:17
"The greatest sacrifice you want is a broken spirit. God, you will gladly accept a heart that is broken because of sadness over sin."

Meanwhile, the door labeled "Judah" led the boys into a long torch-lit hallway full of statues and lined with murals. The statues looked like they were speaking seriously to someone, hands raised and mouths open. Chris paused to look at the murals. "Maybe the pictures will tell us what these guys are saying," he said. "Pretty strange stuff! Who do you think . . . ?"

But Jamal had run ahead. "Come on, Chris," he called, excited. "I can almost smell the treasure—it's so close! We'll beat Niki, for sure!"

Chris ran to join him. "I'm with you!" he cried. There was a musty,

metallic odor to the hallway. Chris imagined that was what piles of gold, silver and jewels would smell like. The boys were so intent on finding the treasure they barely noticed the rest of the pictures along the hallway–paintings showing snow, kings, swords, people feasting and looting.

"Look at that!" Jamal exclaimed, suddenly noticing the looters. "We've got to be close!"

At the end of the hall, something glittered in the torchlight. "All right! There it is! Treasure!" the boys yelled, rushing forward. Just as they reached what appeared to be a

glittering wall of treasure a door clanged shut behind them. They spun around. They were trapped in a dungeon-like room! A solid metal door barred their way back. The room was tiny, dirty and dark, with spider webs everywhere. The glittering they had seen was merely light gleaming off the cobwebs.

"Rats!" Chris said.

"Where?" Jamal jumped.

"No. I mean, we blew it! There's no treasure here!" They looked around the tiny room. The only things in it were two dusty statues tucked into the corners. The boys looked at each other. "What did we do wrong?" Chris asked.

"I'm not sure," Jamal said. "But I know we didn't read the Bible!"

"You're right. This is the first time too. And look where we landed! Boy, we didn't use wisdom, either, did we? Glittering spider webs! Bah!" Chris said in disgust. He paused thoughtfully, "You know? I'm thinking maybe the treasure's not what we think. I mean, maybe it's not gold and stuff, you know? I think it's time to read."

Jamal read the stories Niki was telling Simianne. "Hey, these are about Israel," he exclaimed. He paused to look at Chris with a worried frown, "Maybe Niki was right, after all," he suggested.

"Could be," Chris sighed. "She's pretty smart. But it's too late to go that way, now," he pointed out. "Let's keep reading."

As Jamal read further he said excitedly, "Here's stuff about Judah. Maybe this will help."

Prophets

Prophets in the Old Testament were men and women who knew God and told the people how God wanted them to live. They helped the people keep on track with God and let them know what would happen if they didn't. Listening to the prophets was profitable.

Verse: Isaiah 29:13
"The Lord says, 'These people worship me only with their words. They honor me by what they say. But their hearts are far away from me. Their worship doesn't mean anything to me. They teach nothing but human rules.'"

Isaiah and Jeremiah, Prophets to Judah

(Isaiah 1, 5, 7; Jeremiah 31)

God had warned Israel. He also warned Judah through prophets like Isaiah and Jeremiah: "You have to be willing to change and obey me. If you are, you'll eat the best food in the land. If you don't, you'll be devoured by swords. How terrible it will be for those who say that what is evil is good and what is good is evil, who take money to set guilty people free, and don't treat good people fairly!"

The prophets warned the people of Judah that if they kept sinning, the

king of Babylon would destroy Jerusalem and the temple and take the people as prisoners for 70 years.

But God had a plan to bring his people back to him. He said, "I've loved you with a love that lasts forever.

"The LORD himself will give you a miraculous sign. The virgin is going to have a baby. She will give birth to a son. And he will be called Immanuel. (Immanuel means "God with us.")

"Even though your sins are bright red, they'll be as white as snow."

He promised, "This is the covenant I'll make with Israel. I'll put my law in their minds and write it on their hearts. I'll be their God. And they'll be my people."

The Exile

(2 Kings 25)

The people of Judah didn't listen to the prophets. Everything happened as the prophets said.

Nebuchadnezzar, king of Babylonia, marched out against Jerusalem. All of his armies went with him. He set up camp outside the city. He brought in war machines all around it. He set up ladders and built ramps and towers. He kept the people trapped inside Jerusalem for two years.

There wasn't any food left in the city. So the people didn't have anything to eat. Then the Babylonians broke through the city wall. Judah's whole army ran away at night. But the armies of Babylonia chased King Zedekiah, the king of Judah. They caught up with him in the flatlands near Jericho. All of his soldiers had scattered in every direction.

Nebuzaradan was an official of the king of Babylonia. He set the LORD's temple on fire. He also set fire to the royal palace and all of the houses in Jerusalem. He burned down every important building. The armies of Babylonia broke down the walls around Jerusalem.

So the people of Judah were taken as prisoners. They were taken far away from their own land, just as God said.

"Solomon's temple was destroyed!" Jamal exclaimed, distressed. "But that was where God met with his people!"

"The prophets said he'd still be their God," Chris reminded him. "Even if they were in another country, remember?"

"Oh. Right," Jamal nodded, relieved.

Chris sighed. "We should've paid more attention. We were just after the treasure. The wrong treasure! I wonder where Niki is."

"Aw, don't worry. She's probably better off than we are," Jamal said.

"I hope so. I'm not only worried, though," Chris added with a lop-sided grin. "I'm starved. She has the sandwiches!"

Jamal laughed. "I'm hungry too. We better figure out how to get out of here." The boys examined the only things in the room: two dusty statues. Names were carved into their marble bases. "Isaiah and Jeremiah," Jamal read. "Hey! These are the prophets!" One statue held a scroll.

The other had a jewelled dagger. "Check this out!" Jamal exclaimed excitedly, reaching for the dagger.

"No!" Chris yelled. "Wrong treasure!"

It was too late. The floor dropped out from under Jamal and dumped him into a thigh-deep oozy pool of sludge. "Oh, yuck!" he cried. "And another big mistake!" he sighed, looking up at Chris. "I didn't think, I just grabbed!"

"We read about being devoured by a sword for wrong choices. I guess you were devoured by the floor," Chris laughed. He hauled Jamal out of the muddy mess. When they returned the dagger, the trap-door closed with a firm THUMP.

Chris reached gingerly for the scroll in the other statue's hand. "This probably has God's prophecies. Wha . . . ?" When he lifted the scroll, light began to seep into their dungeon. The wall opposite the door opened silently into a brightly lit cavern. Around a long table at the

Babylonian Archaeology

The ruins of ancient Babylon are located in modern Iraq. The main gate was wide enough for eight fat camels to enter together. Double walls, wide enough to drive chariots on, protected the city. Babylon worshiped gods represented by lions, dragons and bulls. Its streets were paved with slabs carved in their shapes! Talk about animal lovers!

Verse: Isaiah 9:6
"A child will be born to us. A son will be given to us. He will rule over us. And he will be called Wonderful Adviser and Mighty God. He will also be called Father Who Lives Forever and Prince Who Brings Peace."

near end of the cave, low backless couches were piled with cushions. At the far end steam rose from bubbling water. Past the water, just visible through the steam, lions lounged among rocks. Leaning against pillows on one of the couches, Niki and Simianne were eating lunch.

"Boy, are we happy to see you!" Chris declared, making Niki jump. "I'm glad you're OK. Besides, we're hungry!"

"I'm glad to see you too!" Niki said. She saw Jamal covered in mud and burst out laughing. "What happened to you?" Over lunch they told each other their stories.

Finally, waving a hand to indicate the cave, Chris said, "I wonder what all this is about. Let's not blow it again. Let's read."

Daniel and Friends

(Daniel 1)

Many prisoners were taken from Judah to Babylon. God was still working out his plan. He taught his people obedience before he let them go home. The chief official of Babylon chose some prisoners, including Daniel and his three friends, to train for three years. Then they would serve the king.

The king had his servants give these men food and wine from his own table. Because God had given strict rules to his people about eating, Daniel wouldn't eat the king's food.

The official said, "I'm afraid of the king. Why should he see you looking worse than the other young men?"

Daniel said, "Please test us for ten days. Give us nothing but vegetables to eat and water to drink. Then compare us with the young men who eat the king's food." So he tested them for ten days. After the ten days they looked healthy and well fed. In fact they looked better than the young men who ate the king's food.

God gave knowledge and understanding to those four young men. So they understood all kinds of writings and subjects. And Daniel could understand all kinds of visions and dreams. The king didn't find anyone equal to them. Their answers were always the best.

The Fiery Furnace

(Daniel 3)

Daniel and his friends became important men in the kingdom of Babylon.

Later, the king made a huge statue for everyone to worship. Daniel's friends refused. The king said, "Worship the statue I made. If you don't, you'll be thrown at once into a blazing furnace. Then what god will be able to save you from my powerful hand?"

The friends replied, "The God we serve is able to bring us out alive. But even if we knew our God wouldn't save us, we still wouldn't serve your gods or worship the gold statue you set up."

The king was furious! He made the furnace seven times hotter than usual and had the three friends thrown in.

Then King Nebuchadnezzar leaped to his feet. He asked his advisers, "Didn't we tie three men up? Didn't we throw three men into the fire? Look! I see four men walking around. The fire hasn't even harmed them. The fourth man looks like a son of the gods."

He called the friends out. They were fine. Their clothes didn't even smell like smoke! The king was so amazed, he made a law. Anyone saying anything against the God of these three friends would be punished.

Daniel and the Lions' Den

(Daniel 6)

Years later a new king ruled in Babylon. Daniel was the third highest ruler in the kingdom. Other leaders were jealous. They tried to find fault with Daniel's work. But they couldn't. So they made a law. Whoever prayed to anyone except the king would be thrown into the lions' den. Daniel kept praying to God.

When the king heard about it, he was very upset. But the law couldn't be changed, so Daniel was brought out and thrown into the lions' den. The king said, "You always serve your God faithfully. So may he save you!"

As soon as the sun began to rise, the king got up. He hurried to the lions' den. When he got near, he called out to Daniel. His voice was filled with great concern. "Daniel! You serve the living God faithfully. So has he been able to save you from the lions?"

Daniel answered, "My king, may you live forever! My God sent his angel to shut the mouths of the lions. They haven't hurt me at all. That's because I haven't done anything wrong."

The king was filled with joy. He ordered his servants to lift Daniel out of the den. They didn't see any wounds on him. That's because he had trusted in his God.

59

"Imagine sleeping in a lions' den!" Niki said.

"Awesome! Those guys obeyed God and he took care of them!" Jamal added. "But why such hard choices?"

"Good question!" Chris declared. "Let's ask Mom and Dad." With Simianne's help Chris rummaged through Niki's backpack for the mini-phone. The others crowded around so they could hear too.

"God allows us to be tested," Mom responded when Chris asked Jamal's question. "When we trust God even though it's hard, God works things out."

"Daniel's friends said that even if God didn't protect them they'd obey him!" Chris stated. "That would be tough!"

"You're right," Mom agreed. "They obeyed God because they loved him. They knew God loved them too and that his way was best–even though they didn't know how it would turn out. No matter what happens," she added, "God is in charge. His plan is right on track! Nothing can derail it."

"Even the people being taken away from their land?" Jamal asked.

Dad's voice responded, "Yes! God's plan never fails. He was still teaching

160

his people who he was. When God brought them back to their own land again they understood him better."

"But they kept on sinning!" Niki protested.

"They couldn't fully obey him on their own," Mom explained. "They needed help. They needed all of God's plan."

"Sometimes God's lessons are tough," Dad added. "But we can trust that he's in charge. He always looks after his people."

"So we just have to trust, huh?" Chris said. "Thanks." Chris put the phone away and turned to the others. "Where to now?" he asked.

The doors they'd entered by were closed tight. The only exit seemed to be across stepping-stones

scattered through the bubbling water. On the far side, they could see a path leading past the lions lounging among the rocks.

"Those lions look real!" Niki whispered. "But they're not moving."

"We just gotta trust, like Daniel did," Jamal said, jumping from stone to stone. The others followed more slowly. Simianne didn't like the steam and complained from Niki's shoulder. As they approached the lions they saw that they were stone. "See?" Jamal asked. "Safe as puppy dogs."

The kids petted the lions as they climbed past. Simianne held onto a lion's ears and stared into its face, moving her head from one side to the other. Niki laughed as she scooped her up, "It's fake, silly."

The kids followed the path through the rocks to stairs leading up and through a hall of murals. "Let's read," Jamal suggested and opened the Bible to read as they walked.

Punishments of Daniel's time

Babylon had no prisons to punish people for breaking the law. If your "crime" was religious, you died by facing one of their 'gods'–lions, dragons (fire) or bulls. If the "crime" was serious but not religious, they had other punishments, but the results were the same–death.

Verse: Daniel 6:27
"(God) sets people free and saves them. He does miraculous signs and wonders. He does them in the heavens and on the earth. He has saved Daniel from the power of the lions."

The Return

(Ezra 5–6; Nehemiah 4, 6, 8, 10)

God promised his people Israel that they would return to their land.

The people returned in groups over many years. They worked hard. They rebuilt Jerusalem and the temple. Then they rededicated themselves to God's Law.

Important men led each group of people. Zerubbabel and Jeshua began to rebuild the house of God in Jerusalem. The prophets of God were right there with them, helping them. The people finished building the temple. When it was set apart, the people of Israel celebrated with joy.

Nehemiah helped the people rebuild the wall of Jerusalem. Enemies tried to stop them. So those who carried supplies did their work with one hand. They held a weapon in the other. Each of the builders wore his sword at his side as he worked. So the city wall was completed.

When everything was ready, Ezra, a priest and teacher, read from Scripture. He read the Law to them from sunrise until noon. And all the people paid careful attention. They promised to follow the Law of God. They promised to obey carefully all the commands, rules and laws of the LORD.

So God's people returned to their land.

163

"Your Dad was right," Jamal said. "The Jews made it back to their land. God gave it to them twice!"

"Hey, guys, look where we are!" Niki called from up ahead. "It's Solomon's room! We're back where we started from this morning!" The boys followed Niki through an open doorway and dove onto a pile of cushions nearby. The kids had come out from behind a wall panel with a mural of people rebuilding a city.

"This morning seems like a long time ago," Jamal declared.

"Hey, Niki," Chris said, "I'm glad you were OK on your own. I was worried about you. And," he grinned, "not just because you had our lunch!"

"I should've waited for you to figure it out," Niki admitted ruefully. "But I wanted you to think I was smart."

Chris was surprised. "Of course I think you're smart! You've figured out lots of things in here." Niki grinned at her brother's praise.

"Um, Chris," Jamal said, looking sheepish, "thanks for getting me out of that pit."

"You would have helped me, right?"

"Of course!"

"That's what friends are for," Chris declared. "Let's not get separated again. Let's use wisdom and stick together from now on, OK?"

"Yeah!" Jamal and Niki chorused. They all jumped up and high-fived each other. "All for one and one for all!" Simianne put her little hand up too.

"Hey! It's like when the Israelites came back," Jamal added. "They all worked together."

Chris nodded as he sat back down. "I've been thinking. Look at all the people we've learned about: Joseph, Moses, Daniel. I want to be like them!"

"Me too!" Jamal declared. "I want to be like David. He was awesome!"

"King Jamal," Niki laughed. "Who should I be like? I know! Deborah! She was a great leader!" She paused. "I wonder if there were other great women in the Bible besides her and Ruth."

"Let's ask!" Chris suggested, getting out the mini-phone. "Hi, Mom!" he said. "We've read about a lot of men God chose for his plan . . ."

" . . . but only two women," Niki interrupted. "God chose other women besides Deborah and Ruth, right?"

"Absolutely!" Mom said. "Don't forget that God chose Sarah for his plan along with Abraham. There were women prophets too. And a woman saved the whole Jewish nation!"

"God chooses all kinds of people for his plan–men, women, girls and boys," Dad put in. "We're all equal before him. Read Esther!"

Israel's Return

God said the Jews would be exiled for seventy years. Seventy years after Judah's defeat, Jews had returned and rebuilt the temple. As God had predicted, they were back home! Later, Ezra arrived with other priests to restart temple worship. Then Nehemiah rebuilt Jerusalem. Finally, the people promised to obey God's laws.

Verse: Deuteronomy 11:27
"I'm giving you the commands of the LORD your God today. You will be blessed if you obey them."

Esther

(Esther 4–5, 7)

Not all the Jews returned to their land. Among those who stayed behind was Esther, a beautiful Jewish girl. She became queen in Babylonia. Her cousin Mordecai angered an important man, Haman. So Haman passed a law ordering all the Jews in the kingdom to be killed. Mordecai begged Esther to help.

She said, "There's a law that applies to anyone who approaches the king in the inner courtyard without being sent for. It says they must be put to death. But there's a way out. Suppose the king reaches out his

gold rod toward them. Then their lives will be spared."

Esther went to see the king. He held out the gold rod! Esther invited him and Haman to two banquets. At the second banquet the king asked, "What do you want, Queen Esther? I'll give it to you."

Queen Esther answered, "King Xerxes, I hope you'll be pleased to let me live. That's what I want. Please spare my people. That's my appeal to you." Esther told him about the law.

King Xerxes asked, "Who has dared to do such a thing?"

Esther said, "This evil Haman!"

The king was very angry. He punished Haman. Then he wrote another law that saved the Jews. God used Esther to save his people!

But they missed the point. They focused on lots of little rules instead of the heart of the Law. They even said people couldn't spit on the Sabbath because that would be plowing!

Ha! That would be a pretty small field!

They did have a good focus, though—the Messiah, the leader God had promised would fix everything. The Jews were expecting him. They thought he'd be king and defeat the Romans.

Were they right?

Nope. Now we come to the heart of God's plan. God hadn't spoken to the Jews through a prophet for 400 years! Now he broke his silence. Listen to this.

Mary and Joseph

(Luke 1; Matthew 1)

Long ago, God promised Abraham, Jacob and David that one of their descendants would make things right between people and God. It was finally time.

Everything was ready so God fulfilled his promise.

He sent the angel Gabriel to a virgin named Mary. She was engaged to Joseph. The angel said, "God is very pleased with you, Mary. You'll become pregnant and give birth to a son. The power of the Most High God will cover you. So the holy one that's born will be called the Son of God."

Mary and Joseph had promised to get married. But before they were

married Mary became pregnant by the power of the Holy Spirit. Joseph was a godly man. He didn't know what had happened. So he planned to divorce Mary quietly.

As he was thinking about this an angel appeared to him in a dream. The angel said, "Don't be afraid to take Mary home as your wife. The baby inside her is from the Holy Spirit. She's going to have a son. You must give him the name Jesus. That's because he'll save his people from their sins." Joseph woke up. He did what the angel commanded and took Mary home as his wife.

Not long after this, while Mary was still pregnant, she and Joseph had to go on a journey.

The Birth of Jesus

(Luke 2)

In those days, Caesar Augustus made a law. It required that a list be made of everyone in the whole Roman world. So everyone went to their home towns to be listed.

Joseph and Mary, who was almost ready to have her baby, went also. They went from the town of Nazareth in Galilee to Bethlehem, the town of David. Joseph went there to be listed because he belonged to the family line of David.

Bethlehem was so busy because of Caesar's law that there was no room for Mary and Joseph in the inn.

While they were there, the time came for the child to be born. Mary gave birth to her first baby. It was a boy. She wrapped him in large strips of cloth. Then she placed him in a manger. (A manger is a wooden box that holds food for horses, donkeys and cows.)

Mary and Joseph named the child Jesus. This was the name the angel had given him when his mother became pregnant. Jesus was also called "Immanuel," meaning "God with us," because he was God's Son.

It all happened as the angel said it would.

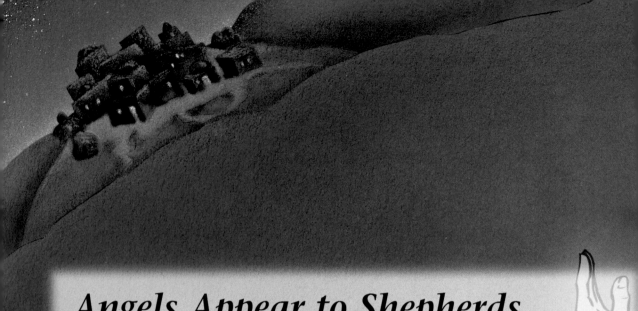

Angels Appear to Shepherds

(Luke 2)

Shepherds looked after their sheep in the hills near Bethlehem. One night an angel of the Lord appeared to them. And the glory of the Lord shone around them. They were terrified.

But the angel said to them, "Don't be afraid. I bring you good news of great joy. It's for all the people. Today in the town of David a Savior has been born to you. He's Christ the Lord. Here's how you'll know I'm telling you the truth. You'll find a baby wrapped in strips of cloth and lying in a manger."

Suddenly more angels appeared, praising God. They said, "May glory be given to God in the highest heaven! And may peace be given to those he's pleased with on earth!"

The angels left and went into heaven. Then the shepherds said to one another, "Let's go to Bethlehem. Let's see this thing that's happened."

The shepherds found Mary and Joseph and the baby. The baby was lying in the manger. After seeing him, the shepherds told everyone what the angel had said about this child. All who heard it were amazed.

But Mary kept all these things like a secret treasure in her heart. She thought about them over and over.

The Wise Men

(Matthew 2)

Later, some Wise Men followed an unusual star to Jerusalem. They believed the star was a sign that a special king had been born. They went to the palace and asked, "Where is the child who has been born to be king of the Jews?"

When King Herod heard about it, he was very upset. He wanted to be the only king. He called the chief priests and the teachers of the law. He asked them where the Christ (or Messiah) was to be born.

"In Bethlehem in Judea," they replied.

Herod said to the Wise Men, "As soon as you find him, bring me a report."

The Wise Men went on their way. The star they had seen stopped over the place where the child was. The Wise Men saw the child with his mother Mary. They bowed down and worshiped him. They gave him gold, incense and myrrh.

But God warned them in a dream not to go back to Herod.

When the Wise Men had left, Joseph had a dream. An angel of the Lord appeared to him. "Get up!" the angel said. "Take the child and his mother and escape to Egypt. Stay there until I tell you to come back. Herod wants to kill the child." So Joseph took Mary and the child to Egypt. They returned after Herod died.

Later that night the family talked around the fire. "I'm glad God told shepherds about the baby first!" Niki said.

Chris asked, "Why didn't he tell the San . . . San . . ."

"Sanhedrin. God wanted us to know his plan was for everyone, not just religious leaders," Dad explained. "And the Wise Men he told weren't even Jews!"

"Do you mean," Jamal asked, "God's big plan was a *baby*?"

Dad laughed. "Exactly. God does things his own way!"

"It's getting late," Mom said. "The rest of the plan will have to wait."

The next morning, back in the Globe Room with Digger, the kids searched for clues from the stories they'd read the evening before. Chris examined the globe. "Look at this map," he called to the others. "If I remember . . . I think this is the Roman empire from the time of Jesus."

Jamal looked over Chris's shoulder. "I think you're right."

"The Romans were important for God's plan," Niki reminded them. "Maybe it's a clue." She looked on the floor around the globe. "Here's another map!" she called.

"Let's match them and see what happens," Jamal suggested. They turned the globe until the two maps matched up. A whirring noise drew their eyes to the ceiling. "Whoa!" Jamal exclaimed. "The whole thing's moving!" A huge mobile of stars and planets hanging from the dome above the globe was slowly turning. A large star on the mobile moved slowly across the dome.

"Like the Wise Men saw!" Niki breathed, following the star. It disappeared through a hole high up in the wall. A second later there was a soft THUNK and a panel below the hole slid back. The kids went through into a room like a stable. In the center was a life-sized nativity scene.

"Like your folks read," Jamal said. "It must've been important for a special star! But, a baby?"

Jesus Fulfills Prophecies

Only God knows the future before it happens. The Old Testament predicted things about Jesus hundreds of years before his birth: his birthplace (Bethlehem), his tribe (Judah), where he would minister (the area around Galilee), and how he would teach (parables). And, most importantly, that he would suffer and die for people's sins. Everything happened as predicted. Take God's Word for it!

Verse: Isaiah 7:14
"The LORD himself will give you a miraculous sign. The virgin is going to have a baby. She will give birth to a son. And he will be called Immanuel."

"Hey, Mary kept things in her heart like a secret treasure, Jamal!" Chris remembered, excited.

"What kind of treasure fits in your heart?" Jamal wondered. "Not the one we were looking for!"

On the other side of the nativity scene stairs led down through a small Egyptian room and back up again. The passage walls showed Mary, Joseph and Jesus going to Egypt and then returning. At the top of the far staircase was a library littered with open scrolls and books. In the center of the room a model of a beautiful temple stood on a table.

Niki asked, "What's this got to do with baby Jesus?"

"Good question," Chris said. "Let's read."

The Boy Jesus at the Temple

(Luke 2)

When they returned from Egypt, Jesus' family lived in Nazareth.

Every year Jesus' parents went to Jerusalem for the Passover Feast. When he was 12 years old, they went up to the Feast as usual. After the Feast, his parents left to go back home. Jesus stayed behind. But they weren't aware of it. They thought he was in their group.

That night Jesus' parents looked for him among their relatives and friends. They didn't find him. So they went back to Jerusalem. After three days they found him in the temple. Jesus was sitting with the teachers, listening and asking questions. Everyone who heard him was amazed at how much he understood. They also were amazed at his answers.

When his parents saw him, his mother said, "Son, why have you treated us like this? Your father and I have been worried. We've been looking for you everywhere."

"Why?" Jesus asked. "Didn't you know I had to be in my Father's house?" But they didn't understand what he meant. He went back to Nazareth with them, and obeyed them. Mary kept all these things like a secret treasure in her heart.

Jesus became wiser and stronger, and more and more pleasing to God and people.

"There's that treasure again," Niki said. "It must have something to do with Jesus."

"Has to," Chris agreed. "Just think! Jesus was our age when he went to the temple, Jamal!"

"Jesus, a kid like us!" Jamal said in amazement.

"Not quite like us," Chris laughed. "There's no way I could go into a huge church and wow the pastors and teachers like he did!"

Jamal said thoughtfully, "You know? I think we're getting close to the treasure we've been searching for. I mean, this is big! God worked for hundreds of years to get things ready for Jesus."

"Yeah, and to teach people what they needed to know so they'd understand it all," Chris added. "So let's see if we can find something here about baby Jesus." They looked around the room. Nothing reminded them of Jesus as a baby. They found statues of two adults, a model of the temple, and a statue of a teenage boy. But no babies.

"Maybe what he was like as a baby wasn't the most important thing," Niki said, discouraged.

"You're right," Chris agreed. "Let's think." He closed his eyes to concentrate. "Hmm. When Jesus was our age, he went to Jerusalem and the temple, right? Then he went back to Nazareth with his folks."

"There!" Jamal yelled. He ran to the statues of the man and woman. On the floor beside them was a space for another statue. "We don't need to find a baby!" Jamal cried. "Jesus was our age when he went to the temple. The boy should be with his parents. Help me!" Together the kids moved the boy statue into place.

There was a loud CRASH. The floor of the room began to tilt toward one corner. In the corner a hole opened. Beyond it a metal ramp dropped out of sight. The kids and dog slid helplessly across the floor toward the waiting chute, Digger yelping all the way. They slid down the chute, gaining speed as they rounded a corner and shot into a pool of water. They landed with a SPLASH! Niki stayed the driest

Jewish Traditions

The Jews have great traditions. The Bar Mitzvah, meaning "son of the divine law" is a special ceremony. It recognizes that a Jewish boy of 12-13 has reached the age of religious duty and responsibility. He's now a "son of the divine law." He can read Scripture in the synagogue. And he must live as a responsible man.

Verse: Luke 2:52
"Jesus became wiser and stronger. He also became more and more pleasing to God and to people."

because she landed on the boys! As
they climbed out, Digger shook
himself, soaking them again and
making them laugh.

"That was fun!" Jamal exclaimed
as they looked around to orient
themselves. They were on a ledge
high on the side of a huge cavern. In
the middle of the cavern a slim tower
of rock rose like a spire until its top
was level with them. A narrow
suspension bridge of planks and rope
led from their ledge across open
space to the rocky spire.

"Whoa!" Chris breathed.

"Is this Nazareth?" asked Jamal,
in awe.

"I don't think so. Here, I'll read,"
Niki suggested.

Jesus' Baptism

(Matthew 3; Luke 3; Mark 1)

Jesus' cousin, John the Baptist, came and preached in the Desert of Judea. He said, "Turn away from your sins! The kingdom of heaven is near." Then God would forgive them.

John's clothes were made of camel's hair. He had a leather belt around his waist. His food was locusts and wild honey. People came from all over to hear John preach and to be baptized by him.

When Jesus was about 30 years old, he came to the Jordan River. He wanted to be baptized by John. But John told Jesus, "I need to be baptized by you. So why do you come to me?"

Jesus replied, "Let it be this way for now. It's right for us to do this. It carries out God's holy plan." Then John agreed.

As soon as Jesus was baptized, he came up out of the water. At that moment heaven was opened. Jesus saw the Spirit of God coming down on him like a dove. A voice spoke to him from heaven. It said, "You're my Son, and I love you. I'm very pleased with you."

This was the beginning of Jesus' public work.

Jesus' Temptation

(Matthew 4; Luke 4)

The Holy Spirit led Jesus into the desert. There the devil tempted him. After 40 days without eating, Jesus was hungry. The tempter said, "If you're the Son of God, tell these stones to become bread."

Jesus answered, "It's written, 'People don't live only on bread. They live on every word that comes from the mouth of God.'"

Then the devil took Jesus to the highest point of the temple. "If you're the Son of God," he said, "throw yourself down. It's written, 'The Lord will command his angels to take good care of you. They'll lift you up in their hands.'"

Jesus answered, "It's also written, 'Do not put the Lord your God to the test.'"

Finally, the devil took Jesus to a very high mountain. He showed him all the kingdoms of the world and their glory. "If you bow down and worship me," he said, "I'll give you all this."

Jesus said, "Get away from me, Satan! It's written, 'Worship the Lord your God. Serve only him.'"

When the devil finished all this tempting, he left Jesus until a better time. Angels came and took care of Jesus.

"We got wet. Like being baptized. But not really," Chris said.

"Yeah," Niki nodded. "Those temptations must've been tough for Jesus."

Jamal agreed. "But he won every time. No contest!"

"I don't understand why God wanted Jesus to be tempted," Chris said. "Let's ask." He started to get the mini-phone out.

Niki glanced around. The bridge was the only way off their ledge. . Suddenly she jumped up and yelled, "Last one across the bridge is a rotten egg!" The boys forgot about looking for the phone and raced after her. Digger was the rotten egg.

He didn't like the bridge at all.

"This is really high!" Chris commented, looking down from the spire. "Like where the devil took Jesus." He paused. "Whoa!" he breathed. "Look at *that*!" The cavern floor was covered with treasure: gold glinted, jewels sparkled, precious things flashed and twinkled. A narrow stairway wound around the spire to the cavern floor.

"The treasure! We'll be rich forever with all that stuff!" Niki exclaimed.

"Hang on. Let's think," Chris said. "I don't trust this. I mean, the devil offered Jesus all the kingdoms of the world. Kingdoms have wealth

and power. Jesus said no to all of it."

"You're right," Jamal sighed. "Every time we've gone for gold and stuff we've gotten into trouble. No more chasing wrong treasure for me!" he concluded.

Niki thought about it. Then she agreed with a sigh. "Jesus said no. He must've had a good reason."

"I think he was saying we should trust God, not money. 'Worship only God.'" Chris quoted. A narrow walkway circled the spire. Chris moved around it until he caught sight of a second rope bridge that had been hidden in the gloom. It led to a book-shaped opening in the far cavern wall. "Jesus quoted from the Bible," Chris observed. "This must be the way out."

"Maybe we could get some treasure and come back up," Niki suggested.

Chris took a deep breath. "We said we'd stick together. What should we do?"

After a pause for thought, Niki said, "I really want *God's* treasure!"

"That's what we've been looking for, right?" Jamal asked. "The 'treasure of God'?" So they all crossed the bridge to the far wall. As they reached it, Jamal looked back. "But we could have . . ." With a loud rumble the steps around the spire disappeared.

"If we'd gone down there," Chris grinned, "we would've been trapped. We made the right choice! Come on."

The kids trooped through the opening into a room full of fishing gear. Nets covered the floor and walls beneath anchors, fishing lines and hooks, traps, sails and ropes. Jamal looked around and got out the Bible with a grin. "Time to read."

Baptism

Baptism is a picture of what happens when we become Christians. It publicly shows that we accept what Jesus did for us. He died, was buried, and rose again so that we could be forgiven. The water over us is a symbol of Jesus' blood washing away our sins. Jesus told us to be baptized and baptize others.

Verse: 1 Corinthians 10:13
"You are tempted in the same way all other human beings are. God is faithful.

He will not let you be tempted any more than you can take. But when you are tempted, God will give you a way out so that you can stand up under it."

The Twelve Disciples

(Matthew 10; Mark 1, 3; Luke 6)

After his temptation in the desert, Jesus returned to Galilee.

One day Jesus was walking beside the Sea of Galilee. He saw Simon and his brother Andrew. They were throwing a net into the lake. They were fishermen. "Come. Follow me," Jesus said. "I'll make you fishers of people." At once, they left their nets and followed him.

Jesus walked a little farther. As he did, he saw James, son of Zebedee, and his brother John. They were in a boat preparing their nets. Right away he called them. They left their father Zebedee in the boat and followed Jesus.

One day, Jesus went out to a mountainside to pray. He spent the night praying. When morning came, he called his disciples and chose 12. From that time on they would be with him. He would also send them out to preach and to heal every sickness.

Simon was one of the disciples. Jesus gave him the name Peter. There were also Simon's brother Andrew, James, John, Philip and Bartholomew. And there were Matthew, Thomas, and James, son of Alphaeus. Also Simon called the Zealot and Judas, son of James. Judas Iscariot was one of them too. He was the one who would later hand Jesus over to his enemies.

"Jesus chose fishermen to be his friends!" Chris said. "I wonder why?"

"Remember the stories of Ruth and David?" Jamal asked. "God chose them because of their hearts, not because they were rich or famous or anything."

Niki was examining the traps and other gear in the room. "This must be what the disciples used for fishing," she guessed. Something moved under her feet. "Uh-oh," she said. "I just . . ." Before she could finish, the net covering the floor rose, lifting them off their feet and tumbling them all together in the middle of it. Digger yelped and whined. The net lifted them like a prize catch of fish through a hole in the ceiling. The hole closed below them with a THUMP and the net released them, dumping them out on the floor.

"Poor Digger," Niki said, throwing her arms around him. "Hard day, huh? Slides, water, bridges–now

his!" She hugged him until his tail wagged again.

The kids looked around. They were in a long, unevenly shaped cavern. One wall of the huge cave was open to the outside, like a window in the side of the cliff. The kids moved to the window in awe and gazed out over the countryside.

"We can see for miles. What a view!" Chris exclaimed.

Jamal pointed to the valley. "Look! It's the Bedouins we visited!"

The phone rang. Mom's voice came through clearly, "How are you doing?"

"Great!" Niki said. "How's the cave?"

"A dead end. We think there's another piece to the map."

"Hey!" Niki exclaimed, remembering the question Chris hadn't had the chance to ask. "A while ago we read how God led Jesus to the desert to be tempted," she explained. "Why did he?" The boys crowded close to hear.

"It was important, Niki," Dad's voice answered. "It shows us Jesus struggled with the same things we do. But he didn't sin. He chose to do things God's way. Because he was tempted, he knows what it's like for us. He can help with our struggles. And he showed how powerful God's Word is when he used it to fight the temptations."

"Yeah! Awesome!" Niki said, understanding. "Thanks."

"Sure. What are you kids up to?" Dad asked.

They all started answering at once. "We found this awesome room . . ." ". . . piles of treasure . . ." ". . . bridges and nets . . ." "Woof!"

Mom laughed, "Whoa! I'm glad you're enjoying yourselves. Madame Zamar and Zareef have invited us for lunch. Are you kids OK for food?"

"Yeah, we're fine," Niki answered. "Thanks." She hung up and they dug out their lunches. They'd brought an old bone for Digger too. Between bites, Niki read from the Treasure Bible. After a while Digger wandered off to explore the parts of the cave away from the window.

Jesus' Temptation

Talk about temptation! Jesus hadn't eaten for 40 days when Satan tempted him with food! Jesus used Scripture to fight every temptation. He was showing us we need to use it too. The Bible is true. Temptation is false. We need to know the Bible so we can resist temptation. Jesus said the truth will set us free.

Verse: Mark 1:17
"'Come. Follow me,' Jesus said. 'I will make you fishers of people.'"

Jesus the Miracle Worker

(Matthew 14; John 6)

One day, a crowd of about 5000 men, plus women and children, was with Jesus, listening to him teach about God. They were hungry. Jesus asked the disciples how they would feed them.

Andrew said, "Here's a boy with five small loaves of bread. He also has two small fish. But how far will that go in such a large crowd?"

Jesus had all the people sit down in groups.

Then Jesus took the loaves and gave thanks. He handed out the bread. He gave everyone as much as they wanted. And he did the same with the fish. When all of them had enough to eat, Jesus said, "Gather the leftover pieces. Don't waste anything." So they gathered what was left over and filled 12 baskets.

Later that night the disciples got into a boat and headed across the lake toward Capernaum. It was dark. Jesus hadn't joined them. A strong wind was blowing, and the water became rough. They saw Jesus coming toward the boat, walking on the water. They were terrified.

But he said, "It's I. Don't be afraid."

When he climbed into the boat, the wind died down. They worshiped Jesus. They said, "You really are the Son of God!"

197

Jesus the Healer

(Matthew 4, 9; Luke 18)

Jesus showed people God loved them. One way he did this was by healing them. People brought all who were ill. Some were in great pain. Some were shaking wildly. Others couldn't move at all. Jesus healed all of them.

One day Jesus and the disciples passed through Jericho. A blind man begging by the road heard that Jesus was walking by. So he called out, "Jesus! Son of David! Have mercy on me!" The people told him to be quiet.

But Jesus stopped. "What do you want me to do for you?" he asked.

"Lord, I want to be able to see," the blind man replied.

Jesus said, "Receive your sight. Your faith has healed you." Right away he could see. He followed Jesus, praising God. All the people also praised God.

Another time, a ruler got down on his knees. He said, "My daughter's just died. But come and place your hand on her. Then she'll live again."

Jesus went with him. When Jesus entered the ruler's house, he saw the flute players and the noisy crowd. He said, "Go away. The girl isn't dead. She's sleeping." But they laughed at him.

After the crowd had been sent outside, Jesus went in. He took the girl by the hand, and she got up!

"Jesus raised that girl from the dead," Jamal said. "Amazing! Hey!" he added suddenly, "remember we read that Mary kept things about Jesus in her heart like treasure? Maybe we . . ."

Digger's bark interrupted him. The kids ran to see what he had discovered. They found him around a bend in the cavern at the edge of a dark chasm. The light from the window barely reached him. The air was musty with the scent of moss and lichens. Jamal tossed a rock over the edge of the chasm. They heard it rattling against the side on its way down. It was a long time before it hit bottom with a faint splash. In the gloom the kids made out words engraved in the wall, "Live by believing, not by seeing."

"Look!" Jamal pointed. "A bridge! Sort of." A solid stone bridge reached halfway across the chasm toward an opening on the other side. It seemed to hang suspended in mid-air. The kids moved cautiously onto it and looked over the end into . . . nothing. It was pitch black.

"This seems to be the way out," Chris muttered. "How do we get across?"

Niki took a breath. "It says to believe, not see. You guys are strong. Hang on to me. I'll reach over with my legs." Chris and Jamal took a firm grip on Niki as she slid her feet over the edge. Her toes hit stone almost right away. "There's something . . ." she began. Digger jumped off the edge past her. "No!" she yelled. But he landed beside her and started licking her face. "Well," she laughed. "I guess you believed!" She turned to the boys. "The rest of the bridge is here! It's just invisible or something. Talk about believing without seeing! Come on!"

The boys joined Niki and Digger. "It's painted black!" Jamal announced, nose almost touching the stone.

The kids crossed the bridge to the opening. A passage led them back to the Globe Room. "Whew!" Chris said. "I'm glad to see this place again!"

"What now?" Jamal asked. A shadow touched his face. He looked up.

Wild Miracles

Talk about wild miracles! The Bible is full of them: creation, parting seas, bread and fire from heaven, people raised from the dead, water becoming wine, the sun standing still . . . And God hasn't changed. He still does great miracles when we trust him. When people pray, God acts. Isn't he awesome?

Verse: Ephesians 3:20
"God is able to do far more than we could ever ask for or imagine. He does everything by his power that is working in us."

"Hey, someone's at the fish pond." Vaguely, through the skylight, they could see someone running a hand through the water. Putting the Bible back they ran to see what was up. The adults and Simianne were just finishing lunch.

"Hi!" Chris called as he approached them. "We thought that was you! We've been reading about miracles," he added. "The things Jesus could do were amazing!"

"The miracles were signs that Jesus was truly God's Son. He had to be God to fulfill the plan," Mom explained.

"Jesus was also a great teacher. Why don't we read about him together?" Madame Zamar suggested, fishing a Bible out of her bag.

Jesus the Teacher

(Matthew 4–5, 7, 22)

Large crowds followed Jesus. His teaching was different than they were used to. Jesus went up on a mountainside to teach.

"Blessed are those who are spiritually needy. The kingdom of heaven belongs to them. Blessed are those who are sad. They'll be comforted. Blessed are those who are free of pride. They'll be given the earth. Blessed are those who are hungry and thirsty for what's right. They'll be filled. Blessed are those who show mercy. They'll be shown mercy. Blessed are those whose hearts are pure. They'll see God. Blessed are those who make peace. They'll be called children of God. Blessed are those who suffer for doing right. The kingdom of heaven belongs to them.

"You're the light of the world. Let your light shine in front of others. They'll see the good things you do and praise your Father in heaven.

"Love your enemies. Pray for those who hurt you.

"Don't judge others. Then you won't be judged.

"'Love the Lord your God with all your heart and soul. Love him with all your mind.' This is the most important commandment. The second is like it. 'Love your neighbor as you love yourself.'"

Parables—The Wise Builder

(Matthew 7, 13; Luke 8)

Jesus taught using stories called parables. He didn't say anything to the crowd without telling a story. That's how the words spoken by the prophet came true. He said, "I'll tell stories. I'll speak about things that were hidden since the world was made."

Jesus' disciples asked him why he used stories.

He said, "You've been given the chance to understand the secrets of God's kingdom. But to outsiders I speak using stories. In that way, 'They see, but they will not know what they're seeing. They hear, but they will not understand.'"

Jesus meant that those who wanted to understand his stories and teaching would understand. But those who didn't would just hear a story.

He said, "Everyone who hears my words and puts them into practice is like a wise man. He builds his house on the rock. The rain comes down. The water rises. The winds blow and beat against that house. But it doesn't fall. It's built on the rock.

"But everyone who hears my words and doesn't put them into practice is like a foolish man. He builds his house on sand. The rain comes down. The water rises. The winds blow and beat against that house. And it falls with a loud crash."

Parables–The Good Samaritan

(Luke 10; John 4)

One day an authority on the law put Jesus to the test. He asked, "What must I do to be saved?" Jesus told him to obey the greatest commandments–to love God and his neighbor.

The man asked, "Who's my neighbor?"

Jesus replied, "A man was going from Jerusalem to Jericho. Robbers attacked him. They stripped him and beat him, leaving him almost dead. A priest was going down that same road. When he saw the man, he passed by on the other side. A Levite (temple-worker) also came by and did the same.

"But a Samaritan came." (Jews don't have anything to do with Samaritans.)

Jesus went on, "When he saw the man, he felt sorry for him. He went to him, poured olive oil and wine on his wounds and bandaged them. Then he put the man on his own donkey. He took him to an inn and took care of him. The next day he gave two silver coins to the owner of the inn. 'Take care of him,' he said. 'When I return, I'll pay you for any extra expense you may have.'

"Which of the three was a neighbor to the man attacked by robbers?"

The man replied, "The one who felt sorry for him."

Jesus told him, "Go and do as he did."

Parables—The Seeds

(Luke 8)

People loved to hear Jesus teach.

A large crowd gathered around Jesus. As they gathered, he told a story. He said, "A farmer went out to plant his seed. He scattered the seed on the ground. Some fell on a path. People walked on it, and the birds ate it up. Some seed fell on rocky places. When it grew, the plants dried up because they had no water. Other seed fell among thorns. The thorns crowded out the plants. Still other seed fell on good soil. It produced a crop 100 times more than the farmer planted."

Jesus' disciples asked what the story meant.

"The seed is God's message. People on the path are those who hear. But the devil takes the message from their hearts so they won't believe. Those on the rock hear the message and receive it with joy. But they have no roots. When put to the test, they fall away from the faith. The seed among thorns stands for those who hear the message but are choked by life's worries, riches and pleasures. They don't reach full growth.

"But the seed on good soil stands for those with an honest heart. They hear the message and keep it in their hearts. They remain faithful and produce a good crop.

"So be careful how you listen."

"The parables Jesus told weren't just stories," Dad said. "They were lessons about God that taught people how to live. Jesus also taught that when we understand something about God or how he wants us to live, we're responsible to do it."

Niki looked at the boys. "We've sure been learning a lot! Now I guess we have to do what we've been learning."

"That's right, Niki," Mom nodded. "Everything Jesus taught, everything you've been learning, is still true today. Remember, Jesus understands what we're learning and how hard it can be to live it. He'll help when we ask."

Niki smiled in relief, "Good!"

"Can you explain what the stories mean?" Jamal asked.

"The one about building on the rock," Chris said thoughtfully, "must mean that doing what Jesus said is wise."

"Exactly. Yes," Zareef agreed with a smile. "The story about the Samaritan teaches us to love and help anyone in need. Jews and Samaritans hated each other. That is why Jesus used a Samaritan in his story. He taught that even your enemy is your neighbor and should be loved."

"Even bullies at school?" Niki asked.

Zareef nodded. "Exactly! Yes! Everyone!"

"In the last story," Madame Zamar continued, "Jesus taught that we must hold on to what we learn. We should keep it in our hearts. Then, like the good seeds, we'll grow and produce a crop."

Jamal smiled. "There's no way I'll forget what I'm learning here!"

The kids sat by the fish pond, running their hands through the water. It was peaceful resting in the sun. A soft breeze carrying the faint scent of flowers tickled their faces and ruffled their hair. Simianne and Digger curled up together at one end of the pond to sleep.

Jamal looked thoughtful. "But how did Jesus learn the things he taught?"

"He was God's Son, Jamal," Dad explained. "That means he was with

---

Names of Jesus

You know how someone's name or title tells you a lot about them? Well, Jesus has lots of titles. See what they tell you about him: "Wonderful Counselor," "Man of Sorrows," "Prince of Peace," "Mighty God," "Savior," "Lamb of God," "King of Kings."

Verse: John 21:25

"Jesus also did many other things. What if every one of them were written down? I suppose that even the whole world would not have room for the books that would be written."

God long before he was born here on earth to Mary. Then, as a boy and man, he studied the Scriptures. And he prayed a lot, talking to his Father. Sometimes he prayed all night!"

"Prayer must be important!" Niki said. "Did Jesus teach about it too?"

"He sure did!" Mom said. "He said prayers should come from the heart."

"Jesus taught his disciples to pray," Madame Zamar added. "Some people call that prayer 'The Lord's Prayer.'"

"Shall we read what Jesus said about prayer?" Zareef asked. When the kids nodded eagerly, Madame Zamar handed Zareef the Bible.

The Lord's Prayer

(Luke 11; Matthew 6–7)

Jesus taught people to pray quietly, in private. Jesus said, "Your Father knows what you need even before you ask him.

"Ask, and it'll be given to you. Search, and you'll find. Knock, and the door will be opened. All who ask will receive. All who search will find. And the door will be opened to all who knock.

"Suppose your children ask for bread. Which of you will give them a stone? Suppose they ask for a fish, which of you will give them a snake? Even though you're evil you know how to give good gifts to your children. How much more will your Father in heaven give good gifts to those who ask him!"

One day Jesus was praying. When he finished, one of his disciples said, "Lord, teach us to pray."

Jesus said, "This is how you should pray. 'Our Father in heaven, may your name be honored. May your kingdom come. May what you want to happen be done on earth as it is in heaven. Give us today our daily bread. Forgive us our sins, just as we've forgiven those who sin against us. Keep us from falling into sin when we're tempted. Save us from the evil one.'"

213

On the castle wall birds sang as if the people below were paying guests, there only to listen to them. A lizard with a bright orange head lay on a wide stone, basking in the sun. In the song-filled courtyard the kids thought about what Zareef had read.

"We know the 'ask and you'll find' verse!" Jamal told the adults, smiling.

"And everyone knows the Lord's Prayer!" Niki added.

"Sometimes we say it without even thinking about what it means, though," Dad said. "When we pray, God is more interested in what's in our hearts than in the words we use. Each sentence in the Lord's Prayer teaches us something about prayer. Remember how it starts? We begin by calling God our Father. We come to him like children and we know he'll hear us."

"Praying for God's name to be honored," Mom continued, "is praying that he'll be known for who he really is: the Creator of everything, the God of truth who is loving and holy and just."

Zareef waved his arms, excited. "Then we pray that God's plans for his kingdom will happen, that what he wants will take place in the world and in our lives. He made us. He knows what is best for us. Yes? After

we tell God that we want what he wants, we ask him to make sure we have all that we need to live."

"The next part is all about forgiveness," Madame continued. "God forgiving us, and us forgiving others. God has forgiven us a great deal. We need to follow his model and forgive others."

"Then," Dad concluded, "we ask God to keep us from things that'll lead us away from him and to keep us safe from our enemy, Satan."

"Then what?" Chris asked. "It just happens?"

Dad laughed. "Sort of. It's like planting a seed. We know something's happening to the seed even though we can't see it. At the right time, up comes the plant. In the same way, we trust God to be 'growing' our prayers. At the right time, in God's way, the answer comes."

"Being here is an answer to prayer that happened at just the right time," Mom added. "We prayed that you kids would get excited about the Bible. And now look at you!"

The kids grinned at each other. They realized Mom was right.

"Why don't we pray right now?" Dad suggested.

"Sure!" the kids chorused.

Everyone gathered around as Dad began. "Father, thanks for answering our prayers and getting the kids excited about your Word. Thanks for loving us and being so good to us. Keep teaching us about you. In Jesus' name, amen."

Answered Prayers

Watching God answer prayer is an amazing thing! It's awesome! Keep a prayer journal. Write down your prayers, then write how and when God answers them. Talk to your parents and friends too. Write down their answered prayers. You'll be amazed at what God does!

Verse: Philippians 4:6
"Don't worry about anything. Instead, tell God about everything. Ask and pray. Give thanks to him."

It was time for Mom and Dad to get back to work. Digger decided he'd had enough of the castle with its bridges and slides and nets, and left with them. Thinking about Jesus' stories, the kids and Simianne got the Treasure Bible and returned to the Globe Room. They looked around carefully.

Suddenly Jamal shouted, "Check out this floor! It's from Jesus' stories." He pointed to a trail of floor tiles painted with scenes from the parables: birds pecking at seeds, seeds among rocks, men walking by another man who was hurt. They followed the tiles to a table in a corner. It held a miniature sculpture of a rocky crag above a sandy beach. Half buried in the sand was a tiny house.

"Silly builder," said Niki, dusting off the house. "He should've built on the rock."

"Just like the parable," Chris commented. As he spoke, Niki placed the little house on the rocky crag. CLICK! Beside them a large painting of Jesus praying swung out. Behind it rose a wide, dimly lit stairway. Simianne clutched Jamal's neck as they climbed. As the kids reached the corner a few steps up, the painting closed behind them.

In the sudden darkness Niki jumped, "What's that?"

Faint light trickled around another corner ahead. A statue in Roman armor stood on the landing, sword drawn. All up the dim stairway statues of soldiers looked ready to attack. Others blocked the way. "They don't want us here," Chris said, ducking under a sword held across the passage. The kids squeezed past the statues and around the corner. Light streamed through a doorway opening onto a beautiful garden. A fountain sparkled and chuckled in the center of a pond. Bright flowers filled the air with their fragrance.

Butterflies were everywhere. Frogs croaked. Birds sang.

The children sat on the grass by the fountain and thought about what they had just learned about prayer. After a while Jamal said, "Those soldiers were cool. But why were they there? Things in here usually mean something." He got up and started wandering around.

"They were like people trying to keep us from following God," Niki suggested.

"I wonder," Chris said thoughtfully. "I think there's more to it."

"Look at all these butterflies!" Jamal called, distracted. "Hey! A cocoon!"

"It's what butterflies come out of, right?" Niki asked excitedly, joining Jamal.

"Uh-huh. First they're caterpillars!" Jamal explained. "My teacher said it's like they're born twice."

"It's pretty amazing," Chris agreed. "Hey! Jesus talked about being born twice!" He quickly got out the Bible.

Times and Places to Pray

Prayer is conversation with God. That's amazing because it means that anywhere you can talk or think, you can pray. And that's just . . . everywhere!

You can pray in bed (or under it!), at school, or even the next time you're taking out the garbage! Anytime, anywhere, about anything!

Verse: 1 Thessalonians 5:16-18

"Always be joyful. Never stop praying. Give thanks no matter what happens. God wants you to thank him because you believe in Christ Jesus."

Nicodemus

(John 3)

There was a Pharisee named Nicodemus, one of the Jewish rulers. He came to Jesus at night and said, "We know you're a teacher from God. We know that God is with you. If he weren't, you couldn't do the miraculous signs you're doing."

Jesus replied, "What I'm about to tell you is true. No one can see God's kingdom without being born again."

"How can I be born when I'm old?" Nicodemus asked. "I can't go back inside my mother! I can't be born a second time!"

Jesus answered, "No one can enter God's kingdom without being born through water and the Holy Spirit. People give birth to people. But the Spirit gives birth to spirit. You shouldn't be surprised when I say, 'You must all be born again.'"

"How can this be?" Nicodemus asked.

"You're Israel's teacher," said Jesus. "Don't you understand these things?

"God loved the world so much that he gave his one and only Son. Anyone who believes in him won't die but will have eternal life. God didn't send his Son into the world to judge the world. He sent his Son to save the world through him."

Opposition to Jesus

(John 7, 11)

Many people put their faith in Jesus. They said, "Will the Christ do more miraculous signs than this man?"

The Pharisees heard the crowd whispering this about him. This made the chief priests and Pharisees angry. They sent temple guards to arrest Jesus.

Jesus spoke in a loud voice. "Let anyone who is thirsty come to me and drink. Does anyone believe in me? Streams of living water will flow from inside the one who believes." He meant the Holy Spirit.

When the people heard him, some said, "This must be the Prophet we've been expecting." Others said, "He's the Christ." Others asked, "Doesn't Scripture say the Christ will come from David's family? From Bethlehem?"

Finally the temple guards went back. The leaders asked, "Why didn't you bring him in?"

"No one ever spoke the way this man does," the guards replied.

"You mean he's fooled you also?" the Pharisees asked.

Nicodemus, who had gone to Jesus earlier, spoke. "Does our law find people guilty without hearing them first?"

They replied, "Look into it. You'll find that a prophet does not come out of Galilee." Then the Jewish rulers began planning to kill Jesus.

221

Jesus and the Children

(Matthew 18–19; Mark 10)

People were bringing little children to Jesus. They wanted him to place his hands on the children and pray for them. But the disciples told the people to stop.

When Jesus saw this, he was angry. He said to his disciples, "Let the little children come to me. Don't keep them away. God's kingdom belongs to people like them. What I'm about to tell you is true. Anyone who won't receive God's kingdom like a little child will never enter it." Then he took the children in his arms. He put his hands on them and blessed them.

Later, the disciples were trying to figure out which of them was the most important. They asked Jesus, "Who's the most important person in the kingdom of heaven?"

Jesus called a little child over to him. He had the child stand among them. Jesus said, "What I'm about to tell you is true. You need to change and become like little children. If you don't, you'll never enter the kingdom of heaven. Anyone who becomes as free of pride as this child is the most important in the kingdom of heaven. Anyone who welcomes a little child like this in my name welcomes me."

Rubbing Simianne behind the ear, Jamal asked, "Jesus was the Son God gave, right? What does it mean, whoever believes in him?"

"Whoever believes that Jesus really was God's Son," Chris answered. "And that he did what the Bible says . . . did God's plan, I guess."

"Do you think we're getting near the end of the plan?" Niki asked.

"I think so," Chris said. "I think it has something to do with the rulers wanting to kill Jesus."

Suddenly Jamal yelled, "Smell that? Fresh bread! Come on!" The kids followed the scent across the garden. A doorway in the far corner led to a winding stairwell. Sacrifices, altars, lambs and goats were painted on the walls on the way down. The stairs ended behind the altar at the end of the Globe Room.

Zareef was standing nearby with a cup and a fresh loaf of bread. "Ah, so you ound your way," he smiled, putting his things on the altar.

"What's all this about, Zareef?" Chris asked, pointing to the altar.

"Altars like this are where the Jews offered their sacrifices," Zareef replied. "The Bible teaches there can be no forgiveness without blood, yes?"

The kids nodded. "The Passover taught us that," Niki responded.

"Do you know how often the Jews offered sacrifices?" Zareef asked.

Chris frowned, "Passover was every year . . . but they offered other sacrifices too."

"Good. Correct. The blood of their sacrifices covered their sin only for a short time, yes? So a new sacrifice was needed. A permanent one. You see? With sins completely covered, people could be with God again, just like before Adam and Eve sinned."

Chris nodded. "I think I understand. Sin separates us from God. So if our sins are covered, we can be with God again."

Zareef grinned, pleased. "Exactly. Also, God wants his people to obey him. God promised to be the Israelites' God. They were to obey the Law and be his people. This was a covenant that God made with them."

"But they kept sinning and serving other gods," Niki protested.

"Exactly, yes. So a new, better covenant was needed. A new promise. The prophets said God would make a new covenant and write his law on people's hearts. With God's ways in their hearts people could obey him more easily. So–the new sacrifice would take care of sins, and people would obey God from their hearts." Zareef smiled. "Jesus talked of this new sacrifice to his disciples. Listen." He took the Treasure Bible from Niki and began to read.

Covenants

A covenant is a commitment between two groups of people. There are two main covenants in the Bible.

	Old Testament Covenant	New Testament Covenant
Between:	God and Jews.	God and all people.
Sealed by:	God's promise, people's sacrifices.	Jesus' sacrifice and resurrection.
Required:	Obedience to the Law.	Acceptance of Jesus, obedience to God.
Achieved by:	People's efforts.	God's Spirit in us.
Result:	Temporary forgiveness, God's presence among them.	Eternal forgiveness, God's presence within us.

Verse: Mark 10:14-15
"Let the little children come to me. Don't keep them away. God's kingdom belongs to people like them. What I'm about to tell you is true. Anyone who will not receive God's kingdom like a little child will never enter it."

The Lord's Supper

(John 13; Luke 22)

Jesus showed his disciples how much he loved them. In an upper room, just before the Passover Feast, he took off his outer clothes and wrapped a towel around his waist. He washed his disciples' feet and dried them with the towel. "Do you understand what I've done for you?" Jesus asked. "I, your Lord and Teacher, have washed your feet. So you also should wash one another's feet."

Jesus said, "I've really looked forward to eating this Passover meal with you before I suffer." Then Jesus took bread. He gave thanks and broke it.

He handed it to them and said, "This is my body. It's given for you. Every time you eat it, do it in memory of me."

After the supper Jesus took the cup. He said, "This cup is the new covenant in my blood. It's poured out for you."

Later, Jesus' spirit was troubled. He knew he was going to be betrayed. So he said, "One of you is going to hand me over to my enemies."

His disciples asked who it was. Jesus said, "It's the one I'll give this piece of bread to." He gave it to Judas Iscariot, son of Simon. Jesus told him, "Do quickly what you're going to do."

Judas went out. And it was night.

"These things," Zareef said as he pointed at the cup on the altar and broke the small loaf of bread in half, "represent Jesus' blood and body, which he was going to offer as a sacrifice to God for our sins. That is the reason Jesus came to earth," he explained. "It was God's plan all along to offer his own Son . . ."

"Like Abraham offered Isaac," Niki broke in excitedly.

"In a way," Zareef replied. Simianne jumped to Zareef's shoulder. He petted her as he continued. "But God's Son would be the one sacrifice needed to pay for all sins for all time. Because of

Jesus' death and blood we could be forgiven. And we could be with God again."

Jamal whistled in amazement that God would love people so much he'd let them kill his Son. "But," he turned to Chris and Niki and whispered, "I thought God's plan led to his treasure?"

"Me too," Niki admitted.

"It still could," Chris suggested. "If Jesus was his treasure . . ." He turned back to ask Zareef. But once again Zareef was gone. This time Simianne was gone with him.

The kids decided to call it a day. They put the Bible back and headed

down to the dig. They found their parents cleaning up from the day's work while Digger rested under the table.

"What's up?" Dad asked. "You look like you lost your best friend!"

"Zareef told us about God making a new covenant with people and needing a permanent sacrifice for sins," Chris explained. "That's Jesus, right? But how?"

"Do you remember the reason for the first Passover in Egypt?" Dad asked. "People killed a lamb and put its blood on their doors so God's angel would pass over them and not kill the oldest child, right?" The kids nodded. "Jesus was going to be the Passover lamb killed for everyone. When people put his blood on the doors of their hearts God 'passes over' them when he judges sin. He forgives them. Jesus died so that we could live, just as the Passover lamb died so the oldest child could live."

Jamal heaved a sigh. "I know it's good," he said, "but it feels sad."

"Remember the whole reason," Mom said. "Jesus died so we could have a close, special relationship with God again. That's what God's plan is all about! No more being separated from God like Adam and Eve and everyone since the first sin!"

"So Jesus really did die, huh?" Jamal asked. He already knew the answer. He just kept hoping he was wrong.

Dad put his arm around him. "Yes, Jamal, he did. Let's read it together."

A Better Substitute

In the story of Abraham and Isaac, God provided a ram to replace Isaac so Isaac could live. In a similar way, in the New Testament, God chose Jesus to take our place so that we would not have to die for our sins. Jesus took our place so we could live forever with God.

Verse: John 3:16
"God loved the world so much that he gave his one and only Son. Anyone who believes in him will not die but will have eternal life."

Jesus' Arrest and Trial

(Matthew 26; John 18–19; Luke 22)

Later that night, in the Garden of Gethsemane, Jesus said to his disciples, "Sit here while I pray. My soul is very sad. I feel close to death." He fell to the ground and prayed, "Father, if possible, take this cup of suffering from me. But do what you want, not what I want."

Judas arrived with a large crowd. They arrested Jesus. Jesus knew God could rescue him. But he said, "All this has happened so that the words of the prophets would come true."

All the disciples left him and ran away.

Jesus was taken to the local ruler, Pilate, to be tried. Peter followed him. Someone asked Peter, "You aren't one of Jesus' disciples, are you?" He said, "I'm not." This happened three times. When morning came Peter went outside. He broke down and sobbed, remembering that Jesus had said this would happen.

Meanwhile, the soldiers beat Jesus, put a crown of thorns on his head, and made fun of him. Pilate questioned him, then said to the Jews, "I find no basis for a charge against Jesus." But the leaders turned the people against Jesus. They shouted, "Kill him! Crucify him!" Finally, Pilate handed Jesus over to be nailed to a cross.

Jesus' Death on a Cross

(Mark 15; Luke 23; John 19)

Soldiers brought Jesus to the place called The Skull. There they nailed him to the cross. Jesus said, "Father, forgive them. They don't know what they're doing."

They crucified two robbers with him. One of the criminals made fun of Jesus. He said, "Aren't you the Christ? Save yourself! Save us!"

But the other said, "Don't you have any respect for God? We're being punished fairly. But this man hasn't done anything wrong." Then he said, "Jesus, remember me when you come into your kingdom."

Jesus answered, "Today you'll be with me in paradise."

At noon, darkness covered the whole land. It lasted three hours. Jesus cried out in a loud voice, "My God, my God, why have you deserted me?" Jesus took his last breath.

A Roman commander heard his cry and saw how Jesus died. He said, "This man was surely the Son of God!"

Afterward, Joseph, a follower of Jesus, went to Pilate and asked for Jesus' body. Nicodemus, the man who had visited Jesus at night, went with him. They wrapped Jesus' body in linen cloths. Then they put it nearby in a new tomb cut in the rock.

By the time Dad finished reading, everyone was really quiet. The campfire crackled and shot sparks into the air making the only sound. The night was quiet and still. Even the crickets were silent.

"That's horrible!" Niki said, after a while. "Jesus' friends left him all alone!"

"He didn't deserve to die!" Jamal declared. "He helped people and taught about God and stuff."

"Even Pilate knew he was innocent!" Chris protested.

"It was because he was innocent that Jesus could pay for our sins," Mom said gently. "The result of sin is death. If Jesus had sinned, he would have had to die to pay for his own sins. But he was innocent. He could pay for our sins because he never sinned himself."

"But why would Jesus do that?" Niki asked, snuggling against Mom for comfort.

"Because he and his Father love us that much," Mom answered, putting her arm around Niki. "They really

want to be close to us. This was the only way to make things right again. So Jesus died."

"So that's the plan God was working toward ever since Adam and Eve?" Chris asked. He was thinking of all the people they'd learned about and how each one fit into God's plan.

"That's right," Dad replied. "God took a long time to get things ready. People needed to know that the result of sin would be death. Then God taught them what it would take to live a sinless life. People found out that no matter what they tried, there's no way they could live on their own without sinning."

"God made sure people knew he was a loving God," Mom added. "Then, when everything was ready and he'd taught people what was needed, he finally carried out his plan. He fulfilled his promise of crushing the snake Satan's head . . ."

"I remember that!" Jamal broke in, excited. "He told Adam and Eve that would happen!"

"Exactly!" Mom smiled. "God promised to make a way for us to be with him. He promised Abraham, Isaac and Jacob he would bless the whole world through their descendants. God promised to write his laws on our hearts so we'd obey him with our whole hearts, not just our heads. And then he fulfilled all his promises in Jesus."

"Talk about a long-range plan!" Chris exclaimed.

Jamal frowned, "So, the plan was over? That's the end of Jesus?"

"Not exactly!" Dad said with a grin. "Listen to this!" He opened the Bible and began to read again.

Jesus, The Pure Lamb

Only because Jesus was so pure and sinless could his sacrifice mean so much. For the Passover sacrifice only the whitest, purest lambs were good enough to remove God's judgment. So Jesus, because of his purity, was the only one who could become the pure Passover "Lamb of God who takes away the sins of the world." And he died during the time of the Passover Feast! Perfect timing!

Verse: Isaiah 53:7
"He was beaten down and made to suffer. But he didn't open his mouth. He was led away like a sheep to be killed. Lambs are silent while their wool is being cut off. In the same way, he didn't open his mouth."

Jesus Rises from the Dead

(Matthew 28; Luke 24)

Very early in the morning on the first day of the week, some women went to the tomb.

There was a powerful earthquake. An angel of the Lord came down from heaven. He went to the tomb, rolled back the stone and sat on it. His body shone like lightning. He said to them, "Don't be afraid. I know you're looking for Jesus, who was crucified. He's not here! He's risen, just as he said he would! He said, 'The Son of Man must be nailed to a cross.

On the third day he'll rise from the dead.' Go! Tell his disciples, 'He's risen from the dead.'"

The women told the disciples. They were talking about this when Jesus himself suddenly stood among them. He said, "May peace be with you!"

They thought they were seeing a ghost.

Jesus said, "Why are you troubled? It's really I! Touch me and see. A ghost doesn't have a body or bones. But I do." They were amazed and filled with joy. Jesus said, "This is what I told you while I was with you. Everything written about me in the Law of Moses, the Prophets and the Psalms must come true."

Then he opened their minds so they could understand the Scriptures.

"*Yes!* All right!" The kids leaped to their feet and high-fived everyone in sight, including Digger!

"I knew there'd be a good ending!" Jamal declared.

"That was what made God's plan a real winner!" Mom laughed. "If Jesus had stayed dead, Satan would have won. Death had been Satan's victory ever since Adam and Eve disobeyed. But Jesus beat it."

"Jesus' rising from the dead was the final proof that he was God," Dad added. "No one except God could give life to something dead. He's a *living* God. And now," he continued, "Jesus' sacrifice covers everyone's sin. So, to be close to God all we have to do is . . ."

". . . believe in Jesus!" the kids shouted together.

"That's the end of the plan?" Niki asked.

"Not quite," Mom said. "God's plan has to be explained to people everywhere so they can believe in Jesus too." She paused. "But that can wait. Bedtime."

The next morning the kids and Simianne wandered down the long wing of the Globe Room. A beautiful stained glass picture of Jesus on the cross hung on one wall. Jamal pointed to the picture. "That's what we read about last night," he stated. "Let's check it out."

The kids poked and prodded the picture, looking for a trigger. It swung open silently. They climbed through the opening into a dark, musty hallway. Getting out their flashlights, they went down steep stairs into a lofty cavern. Their lights flashed over a large rocky outcropping in the center. It looked just like the top of a huge skull! "Ooh, creepy!" Niki shivered. Simianne was shivering too.

"It's like the place Jesus died!" Chris said, pointing to three crosses on top of the outcropping. "They put his body nearby. There should be a tomb . . ."

"Up there!" Jamal pointed with his flashlight. Its light illuminated an uneven flight of stairs curving around

Resurrection

Jesus' tomb was sealed and guarded. Was the resurrection real? Some said the Jews or Romans stole Jesus' body. If so they could have produced it to prove the disciples wrong. Some blamed the disciples. But it was impossible to sneak a body past Roman guards. Nobody had the body because Jesus really *did* rise from the dead! Yes, the resurrection was real. It happened!

Verse: 1 Corinthians 15:17, 20
"And if Christ has not been raised, your faith doesn't mean anything. Your sins have not been forgiven . . . But Christ really has been raised from the dead. He is the first of all those who will rise."

the cavern. The kids climbed to the landing at the top. Beside a cave mouth a flat, circular stone leaned against the rock. The kids entered the cave. With a loud RUMBLE the stone rolled along a track behind them and THUNKED into place. Simianne squealed. They were trapped in an empty cave! They shone their lights around, but there seemed no way out.

"Hmm," Chris muttered thoughtfully. "Hey!" he suddenly exclaimed.

"If we turn our flashlights off we'll see if there's any light." The kids followed Chris' suggestion and waited for their eyes to adjust. Soon they could see a thin line of light seeping in around a large stone opposite them. They pushed on the stone as hard as they could. Nothing happened.

"There should be a trigger . . . ," Niki guessed, feeling around the stone.

"Bring the Bible!" Niki said. She'd found an indent in the stone. Chris fished the Bible out of his backpack. It fit the indent perfectly! WHUMP! The ground shook! Grinding noises deafened them! Simianne squealed and clung in panic to Niki. Niki dropped the Bible to comfort her. Finally, everything got quiet. Then the stone rolled aside. Light flooded in. A few steps led up to the Globe Room.

"What was *that* all about?" Jamal asked. The kids rushed up the stairs, forgetting the Bible and Chris's backpack. "The globe's folded back!" Jamal yelled. "Come ON!" They ran to the globe, Simianne still clinging to Niki. Stairs led beneath the globe into a small torch-lit room. The kids raced down the stairs. In the middle of the room was a cross-shaped reflecting pool. Chiselled in the edge of the pool was "God loved the world so much he gave his only Son." On the bottom of the pool they could read, "Behold the Treasure of God!" And cut into a wall was "Treasure's

task now begun, obedience to the Coming One."

With a rumble the globe folded up, trapping them. Chris watched it. Etched on its lower surface was a map of the world. "Hmm. The world . . . ," Chris muttered.

"It says the treasure's here!" Jamal exclaimed. He bent over the water, searching with his eyes. "It's empty," he announced, disappointed.

Simianne leaned over the pool, saw her reflection and jumped in alarm. Niki laughed at her and leaned over the water too.

"Hey, look at this," Chris said, pointing to the pool. "'God so loved the world,'" he quoted. "You can see the world . . . Maybe that's God's treasure . . ."

"I can see me," Niki commented. "Ohhh!" she breathed.

Peculiar Treasure

So—who would you be willing to die for? Anyone? Jesus loved us so much that he gave up all of heaven and even his own life so we would know and love God. He even did this for those who hate him. He truly treasures us!

Verse: 2 Corinthians 5:17
"Anyone who believes in Christ is a new creation. The old is gone! The new has come!"

'I see me, Chris! Maybe I'm God's treasure . . ." Her eyes were huge with the amazing revelation.

The boys looked in the pool. "I think you're right!" Chris said in awe.

"Wow!" Jamal breathed. "Jesus died for *us*! *We're* God's treasure!" The kids stared at each other, mouths open in astonishment. Simianne chattered at them. Jamal said slowly, "God's plan was for *me*! So I could be with him." He paused then stated boldly, "I believe in Jesus and what he did."

Chris grinned. "Me too. I asked Jesus' forgiveness years ago, but I didn't really understand. Now that I know God's plan, it means a whole lot more!" he declared.

"I didn't realize how much God loved me," Niki added. "I like being treasure! We've got to tell Mom and Dad! Where's the phone?"

"In my pack . . . oops," Chris's voice faded. "I left it in the cave."

"Don't panic," Jamal said. "We'll just find our way out. Let's read."

"Oh, no!" Niki wailed. "I was so excited . . . the Bible's in the cave too." After a silence, Niki suggested, "We better pray."

241

Mom and Dad paused in their work when Zareef called to them. "I found this," he said, waving a stone fragment. "Perhaps it is part of your map?"

The Delves eagerly matched the fragment to their pieces of the map. It fit perfectly! "We've been looking in the wrong place!" Mom declared. They all ran with Digger to the cliff. Behind huge vines they found a rectangular cave entrance! As

they entered Zareef handed Dad a large Bible.

"This might be useful," he said mysteriously. Puzzled, Dad took it. Mom, Dad and Digger explored the cave. At the back a steep stairway wound up through the cliff, its walls covered with ancient murals.

"I've seen these before! Ransach sketched them in his journal!" Dad exclaimed as they climbed. The stairs led to an empty torch-lit room. Wall mosaics showed Jesus ascending into heaven. "Tenth century," Dad declared. "We've found Tresor's Caverns!" he shouted, swinging Mom around. Digger barked. A door slammed shut behind them.

"Digger? Dad?" Chris's voice came faintly.

"Chris? Where are you?" Mom called.

"We're trapped! We forgot the Treasure Bible. We need it to get out."

"Zareef gave us a 'Treasure Bible,'" Dad said. Following Chris's advice he found an indent hidden in the mosaic. He fit the Bible's cover into it. THUNK! The wall swung open. Three kids and a monkey tumbled out babbling, "God answered our prayer! We're God's treasure! How'd you get here?"

"God's plan was for *me*!" Jamal declared. "I want to tell him I accept what Jesus did for me. Can you pray with me?"

"Us too!"

"Of course!" Mom and Dad exclaimed, hugging the kids. "Pray after me," Dad said. "Dear God, we know we're sinners. We're sorry. Please forgive us. We believe your Son, Jesus, died for our sins and rose from the dead. We accept what he did for us. We want to be your children. Thanks for loving us and seeing us as your treasure. Help us obey you. In Jesus' name, amen."

As they finished praying Jamal shouted, "I feel *great*! I'm God's treasure!"

Mom laughed, "And now you're all part of his family too."

Later, Chris asked, "How did you guys get here?"

Mom told them. "These are Tresor's Caverns!" she concluded.

"They are?" the kids asked, surprised. "We thought you were looking for old pottery and stuff," Chris explained. "This is an adventure museum!"

"I can see the confusion," Dad confessed with a smile. "How do we get out?"

"We read the Bible," Niki explained. "The story will tell us what to do." So Dad opened the Treasure Bible and read.

Come to God

Did you know? God loves to have kids come talk to him! He wants to be part of your life. Your relationship with God can start right now no matter how old or young you are. God already loves you. He's listening for your voice. Talk to him!

Verse: Romans 10:9-10
"Say with your mouth, 'Jesus is Lord.' Believe in your heart that God raised him from the dead. Then you will be saved. With your heart you believe and are made right with God. With your mouth you say that Jesus is Lord. And so you are saved."

Jesus Returns to Heaven

(Matthew 28; Acts 1; Luke 24)

After Jesus rose from the dead, he appeared to the disciples over a period of 40 days.

He told them, "All authority in heaven and on earth has been given to me. So you must go and make disciples of all nations. Baptize them in the name of the Father, Son and Holy Spirit. Teach them to obey everything I've commanded you. You can be sure I'm always with you, to the very end.

"Don't leave Jerusalem. Wait for the gift my Father promised."

Jesus had told them God would send a gift of the Holy Spirit to help

244

them. He said, "You'll receive power when the Holy Spirit comes on you. Then you'll be my witnesses from one end of the earth to the other."

Jesus led his disciples out of the city. He lifted up his hands and blessed them. While he was blessing them, he left them. He was taken up into heaven.

The disciples worshiped him. They watched until a cloud hid him.

Suddenly two men dressed in white stood beside them. "Men of Galilee," they said, "why do you stand here looking at the sky? Jesus has been taken away from you into heaven. But he'll come back in the same way you saw him go."

With great joy, they returned to Jerusalem.

Pentecost

(Acts 2)

Not long after that, on the Jewish holiday of Pentecost, those who believed in Jesus gathered together. Suddenly a sound like a strong wind filled the house. Something like tongues of fire settled on each of them. They were filled with the Holy Spirit. They began to speak in languages they hadn't known before.

A crowd gathered because of the sound. They asked, "What does this mean?" Some thought the believers were drunk.

Peter explained what was happening. "Here's what the prophet Joel meant. He said, 'In the last days,' God says, 'I'll pour out my Holy Spirit on all people. Your sons and daughters will prophesy. I'll show wonders in the heavens and miraculous signs on the earth. Everyone who calls on the name of the Lord will be saved.'"

"You nailed Jesus to the cross. But God has made him both Lord and Christ."

The people's hearts were filled with shame. They said, "Brothers, what should we do?"

Peter replied, "Turn away from your sins and be baptized in the name of Jesus Christ. Then your sins will be forgiven. You'll receive the gift of the Holy Spirit."

About 3,000 people joined the believers that day.

The Birth of the Church

(Acts 2, 4)

The disciples, now called apostles, helped the new believers. They taught them all about Jesus just as Jesus had told them to. He'd told them to make disciples.

The believers studied what the apostles taught. They shared life together. They broke bread and ate together. And they prayed. All the believers were agreed in heart and mind. They didn't claim that anything they had was their own. They shared everything. There were no needy persons among them. From time to time, those who owned land or

houses sold them. They brought the money from the sales and put it at the apostles' feet. It was then given out to anyone who needed it.

Every day they met together in the temple courtyard. In their homes they broke bread and ate together. Their hearts were glad and honest and true.

The apostles did many wonders and miraculous signs. With great power the apostles continued their teaching. They gave witness that the Lord Jesus had risen from the dead.

They were greatly blessed by God and respected by all the people. Everyone felt that God was near. They praised God.

Every day the Lord added to their group those who were being saved.

"God came with fire before," Niki stated. "When Elijah prayed. And when they finished Solomon's temple, right?"

"Right!" Mom agreed. "This time it was different though. This time God came to people, to live *within* them through the Holy Spirit."

Dad nodded. "Remember Adam and Eve were separated from God? Inside, in their spirits, they died because of sin. God showed the Jews they couldn't keep his laws while they were separated from him. Well, now they weren't separated from him any more. Because of Jesus, their spirits were alive again, 'born again.' God gave them new hearts so that they'd want to obey him out of love. And, by his Spirit, he'd help them do just that."

Chris asked, "He helps us obey too, right?"

"Absolutely. We're his children. He knows we need it," Dad said.

As they talked, the wall to the

oom with the pond had been slowly closing. Now it WHOOSHED shut! Several torches set in brackets on the wall suddenly burst into flame. Digger and Simianne yelped. Mom jumped. "What happened?" she gasped.

"That kind of stuff always happens in here," Niki explained casually.

"Look!" Jamal pointed. Everyone turned to see what had caught his attention. Unlit torches in brackets lined two other walls.

"Let's light them." Chris suggested. "Hey! Like God's fire!" Mom looked puzzled. Chris explained, "Everything in here means something."

"You mean," Mom asked, "lighting these might be like passing on our faith?"

"Hmm, and fire represents the Holy Spirit," Dad added. He reached for a torch. As each torch was lit the group heard a soft whine. As the last torch caught fire the whine became a SQUEAL. A section of the wall without torches on it slid outward.

"Come on!" Niki said, dashing for the opening. A long, narrow, sloping hallway led up to a room crowded with statues of animals and birds. Miniature elephants and life-sized snakes, octopi, pigs, turtles, crocodiles, lizards, and a horse filled the space! Birds stood on perches near the ceiling as if ready to fly. In the center of the room a table was set for a meal.

Digger growled, eyeball to eyeball with a huge stone crocodile.

"Check it out!" Jamal cried as he climbed on the crocodile.

"What's this about?" Chris asked, looking around.

"This looks like . . . ," Dad paused. "Yes! The Jews had strict laws about eating. These are all 'unclean' animals that they were forbidden to eat."

"Then why the table?" Chris asked, puzzled.

"We better read," Jamal suggested with a grin.

God's Presence

God always wanted to be present with his people because he loved them. Sin separated them from God. In the Old Testament God lived near them in the tabernacle and temple. Now, because of Jesus' work, the separation is over. God lives in us! He calls us his temple! You can't get any closer than that!

Verse: Matthew 28:19-20
"So you must go and make disciples of all nations. Baptize them in the name of the Father and of the Son and of the Holy Spirit. Teach them to obey everything I've commanded you. And you can be sure that I'm always with you, to the very end."

Peter and Cornelius

(Acts 10–11)

One day, Peter had a vision. He saw a large sheet being let down to earth with all kinds of animals, reptiles and birds in it. A voice told him, "Get up, Peter. Kill and eat."

"No, Lord!" Peter replied. "I've never eaten anything that isn't 'clean.'"

The voice said, "Don't say anything isn't pure that God has made 'clean.'"

While Peter was thinking about this, the Holy Spirit spoke to him, "Simon, men are looking for you. I've sent them."

The men told Peter, "We've come from Cornelius, the Roman commander. He's a good man who worships God. An angel told him to invite you. He wants to hear what you have to say." So Peter went with the men.

Cornelius said, "We're ready to listen to everything the Lord has commanded you to tell us." While Peter was talking about Jesus, the Holy Spirit came on all who heard. They spoke in languages they hadn't known before. And they praised God.

The Jewish believers were amazed. They had thought Jesus died only for Jews. They said, "So then, God has allowed even those who aren't Jews to turn away from their sins and live."

Saul Believes

(Acts 7–9)

Jews who weren't believers started causing trouble. They had killed Jesus, and now they started killing his followers. Stephen was killed with stones. The stone throwers placed their coats at the feet of a young man named Saul. Saul agreed that Stephen should die.

Saul went to the high priest and got letters to the synagogues in Damascus. The letters allowed him to take believers as prisoners to Jerusalem. Saul approached Damascus. Suddenly a light from heaven flashed around him. He fell to the ground. He heard a voice say, "Saul! Why are you opposing me?"

"Who are you, Lord?" Saul asked.

"I'm Jesus," he replied. "Go into the city." Saul got up. For three days he was blind.

In Damascus there was a believer named Ananias. The Lord called to him, "Ananias! Go to the house of Judas. Ask for Saul. He's praying. In a vision he's seen a man named Ananias come and place his hands on him so he'll see again." Ananias went and placed his hands on Saul. Something like scales fell from Saul's eyes. He could see again. He got up and was baptized.

Saul became one of Jesus' strongest followers.

"I wouldn't have wanted to eat these animals either!" Niki declared.

"By telling Peter it was OK though, God was saying the good news about Jesus was for everyone!" Dad explained. "If it hadn't been for that, we wouldn't be followers of Jesus. We're non-Jews or Gentiles. They would have thought we were 'unclean.'"

"Boy! I'm glad God showed Peter those rules had changed then!" Jamal said. "But why did some of the Jews hate Jesus' followers?"

"Good question," Mom said. "They didn't believe Jesus was God's Son, the Messiah God had promised. They thought Jesus was a fake. So they tried to stop people from following him."

"He wasn't fake though," Niki declared. "How come God chose Saul to be part of his plan?" she asked. "He was a killer!"

"Remember Jacob?" Chris said. "He wasn't perfect, but God chose him."

"Yeah, you're right. God looks at hearts," Niki remembered.

"God had plans for Saul all right," Dad said. "He was going to use him for the next part of his plan. God promised Abraham that all the nations of the world would be blessed through him. Jesus, as Abraham's descendant, fulfilled that promise. But now the task or the job was to get the word out to everyone."

"Hey! The words in the pond room said, 'Treasure's task now begun.' Maybe telling people about Jesus is the task!" Jamal exclaimed, excited.

"Awesome!" Chris agreed. "That's where Saul comes in, right?" Chris wandered across the room and paused by the horse. "I wonder if this is his horse or something," he murmured as he scrambled into the saddle. He lost his balance when Simianne landed on his shoulder. The horse reared back, dumping them both onto the ground. "Oof!" Chris exclaimed. With a creak a section of wall behind the horse opened.

"What now?" Dad asked, startled.

"I guess it was worth it," Chris grinned, dusting himself off. "Come on!" Beyond the opening an arched bridge crossed a small river. Water splashed into the river from

Paul

Paul was born in the Roman town of Tarsus, taught by one of the leading teachers of his time and raised in a wealthy home in Jerusalem. He was intelligent and enthusiastic in everything he did. He also wrote half the books of the New Testament!

Verse: Galatians 3:28
"There is no Jew or Greek. There is no slave or free person. There is no male or female. Because you belong to Christ Jesus, you are all one."

ountains on the walls. The floor on the other side was a huge map with model towns and people scattered across it.

"Amazing!" Mom said, taking it all in. "This is a map of the known world in Paul's time. Look," she pointed excitedly, "the people are dressed exactly right for that era. What a find!" The bridge gave a wonderful view of the whole thing. It ended at a city marked "Antioch."

"Why Antioch?" Jamal wondered.

"Believers were first called Christians there," Dad said. "And that's where Saul, now called Paul, began his missionary journeys. Gather around, kids. Let's read about them."

Paul, Apostle to the Gentiles

(Acts 13–14)

Saul went with Barnabas to Antioch to teach in the church. While the church was worshiping the Lord and fasting, the Holy Spirit spoke. "Set apart Barnabas and Saul for me," he said. "I've appointed them to do special work."

Barnabas and Saul (also called Paul) traveled, telling everyone about Jesus. They went to Jewish synagogues first.

Paul said, "Your sins can be forgiven because of what Jesus has done. Through him everyone who believes is made right with God." Many Jews and non-Jews followed Paul and Barnabas. Other Jews became very jealous.

Paul and Barnabas told them, "We had to speak God's word to you first. But you don't accept it. So we're turning to those who aren't Jews as the Lord has commanded us."

This made the non-Jews glad.

The word of the Lord spread through the whole area. Paul and Barnabas spoke boldly for the Lord. He gave them the ability to do miraculous signs and wonders. In this way the Lord showed that they were telling the truth about his grace.

Paul went on three missionary journeys and started churches in many cities. Later he wrote letters to the churches, teaching them more about being Christians.

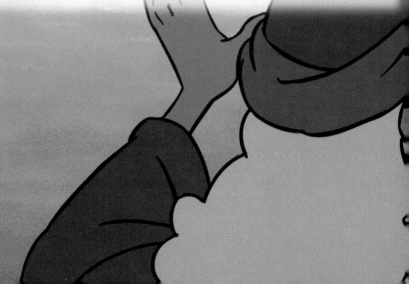

The Jerusalem Conference

(Acts 15)

The believers accepted the fact that anyone could become a Christian. But certain Jews came to Antioch teaching that non-Jewish believers still had to obey the law of Moses and follow the many laws about holy days, cleanliness, work, food and daily life.

Paul and Barnabas argued strongly with them. The church sent them to Jerusalem to see the apostles and elders about this. They met to consider this question.

Peter reminded everyone of Cornelius. He said, "God knows the human heart. By giving the Holy Spirit to non-Jews, he showed he accepted them. He made their hearts pure because of their faith. Why are you testing God by putting a heavy load on believers' shoulders? No! We believe we're saved through the grace of our Lord Jesus. Non-Jews are saved the same way."

James spoke up. "Brothers, we shouldn't make it hard for non-Jews who are turning to God. We shouldn't make them keep the Jewish Law."

They sent men to Antioch with a letter explaining the decision. In Antioch, the men gathered the believers together and read the letter. The people were glad for its message of hope.

Letter to the Galatians

(Galatians 5)

On their first journey, Paul and Barnabas started several churches in the province of Galatia. Later, Paul heard that the people were trying to obey the Jewish Law. He wrote a letter to them with the help of a friend. The letter explained that they were free from the Law. The important thing was to allow God's Spirit to guide them in living a godly life.

"Christ has set us free. He wants us to enjoy freedom. So stand firm. Don't let the chains of slavery hold you again. You were chosen to be free. But don't use your freedom as an excuse to live in sin. Instead, serve one another in love. The whole Law can be found in a single command. "Love your neighbor as you love yourself."

"So I say, live by the Holy Spirit's power. Then you won't do what your sinful nature wants you to do. It doesn't want what the Spirit wants. But if you're led by the Spirit, you aren't under the authority of the law.

"The fruit the Holy Spirit produces is love, joy and peace. It's being patient, kind, good, faithful and gentle and having control of oneself. There's no law against things of that kind.

"Since we live by the Spirit, let's march in step with the Spirit."

"Freedom!" Jamal shouted, tossing Simianne in the air. She grabbed his wrist with her tail and hung on, enjoying herself.

"Obeying the Law's like trying to please God on our own, huh?" Chris said. "Can't happen. We learned that!"

"Exactly!" Dad nodded. "That's what Paul preached." Walking across the map Dad pointed out where Paul had started churches. "Other believers were spreading the message too," he explained. "Amazing!" he added. "If this is accurate . . ." His voice trailed off as he studied the map.

Wandering around in awe Mom found a small prison cell in a far corner. It held a set of inscribed tablets. "A replica of Moses' tablets! This is what Paul was writing about," she called excitedly, entering the cell. "Trying to obey the Law leads to . . ." the door CLANGED shut behind her ". . . bondage. What happened?"

"You gotta be careful, Mom," Niki chuckled, coming over. "Everything means something, remember?" The boys joined her, laughing.

"You entered the Law cell, Lori," Dad said, smiling. "You're in bondage."

"Well," Mom smiled ruefully, "stop enjoying it so much and get me out."

"It'll be . . . keys!" Jamal shouted. He grabbed a large key ring off a hook on the wall. "There's hundreds of them!" They tried several keys. None fit.

"Let's think," Chris said. "What sets us free?"

"Obeying Jesus," Mom answered. "Following his Spirit."

"What would a Spirit key look like?" Jamal asked, going through the ring.

"The Spirit's like fire," Niki said. "Remember?"

"Here!" Jamal held a key up. "See! Shaped like a flame!" The key slid into the lock and turned smoothly. "Now what?" he asked. "How do we get out of here?"

Digger was sniffing along one wall, whining. "What is it, Digger? Is this the way out?" Chris asked. The family searched near him. Hidden in a decorative cross carved in the wall was a cross-shaped keyhole.

"Jesus sets us free!" Chris declared as he and Jamal searched for and found a matching key. The door opened into a long room full of life-sized statues in Roman dress. Half the room was lit by high, narrow windows. The light fell onto laughing, clapping, smiling statues. Little light reached the other half of the room where statues hung their heads and had tears and frowns on their faces.

Jamal pointed to a sad statue clutching jewels. "Wrong treasure!"

"Josh! If I'm not mistaken these are the Jonas statues!" Mom exclaimed. "Jonas described them in his diaries. They've been lost for centuries! Wow!" She paused, looking around the room. "Hmm . . . I think this room must be about Paul's letter to the Romans," she guessed. Mom opened the Bible. As she read, the kids got out their lunch and shared it around.

Transportation

Have you ever ridden a camel or donkey? Or walked several miles? Paul did. He walked thousands of miles. Sometimes he traveled by ship. He had at least three shipwrecks! Walking, he probably covered 16 miles a day. What would take a few hours by car would have taken Paul weeks to travel! Talk about blisters!

Verse: Colossians 1:13
"He has saved us from the kingdom of darkness. He has brought us into the kingdom of the Son he loves."

Letter to the Romans

(Romans 8)

Paul hadn't been to the Roman capital city yet. During his third missionary journey he wrote this letter from the city of Corinth to believers in Rome to encourage them.

"Those who belong to Christ Jesus are no longer under God's sentence.

"I'm now controlled by the law of the Holy Spirit. That law gives me life because of what Christ Jesus has done. It has set me free from the law of sin that brings death. Don't live under the control of your sinful nature. Live under the control of the Holy Spirit. Those who are led by the Spirit of God are children of God.

"We know that in all things God works for the good of those who love him. What should we say then? Since God is on our side, who can be against us? God didn't spare his own Son. He gave him up for us all. Then won't he also freely give us everything else?

"Who can separate us from Christ's love? Can trouble or hard times? No! In all these things we'll do even more than win! We owe it all to Christ, who has loved us. I'm absolutely sure that nothing at all can ever separate us from God's love because of what Christ Jesus our Lord has done."

"God wants only our best!" Dad said when Mom finished reading. "We accept his love and respond with obedience. Obedience is a key task. Then we become more like God wants us to be."

"'Treasure's task now begun, obedience to the Coming One!'" Niki quoted excitedly. "That's what it said in the pond room. We're the treasure. Our job is to get closer to God! He wants to be close to us!"

Jamal grinned. "You're right. Nothing can change God's love! And he helps us because he loves us."

Mom nodded. "We need to ask for his help though. I guess these sad statues didn't," she said pointing to them. "Maybe they tried to live their own way."

Jamal started thinking aloud, "'Obedience to the Coming One,'" he said slowly. Then he jumped up suddenly, scaring Simianne, who leaped for the safety of Niki's arms. "That's it! We have to find something about Jesus. He's the 'Coming One' we have to obey!"

Digger barked eagerly as they split up to search.

"Over here!" Chris called from the far end of the room. "One of these doors." He'd found several doors each with a symbol burned into it–a diamond, a sword, a crown, a lamb, a castle.

"This one," Jamal shouted, opening the door with a lamb on it. They all went through and walked up a cross-shaped ramp.

"Amazing!" Dad said, turning to look back. "Tresor arranged it to show that we must choose to trust Jesus' sacrifice to save us instead of doing things our way. God forgives us when we accept Jesus as the sacrificial lamb. We walk through that, like walking through the 'lamb' door. The ramp takes us up from the place of struggle into a different, better place."

The kids just looked at him quizzically. Finally Niki said, "We told you everything meant something."

The ramp led to a long hallway brightly lit by several windows near the ceiling. It smelled fresh and

Steps to Salvation

1) God loves us and wants a personal relationship with us.
2) But we choose to go our own way and are separated from God because of sin.
3) God sent Jesus to make a way for us to be close to him again.
4) To be reunited with God we must accept Jesus as Lord and Savior.

Verse: Romans 8:14-15
"Those who are led by the Spirit of God are children of God. You didn't receive a spirit that makes you a slave to fear once again. Instead you received the Holy Spirit, who makes you God's child. By the Spirit's power we call God 'Abba.' Abba means Father."

clean. On the walls hung beautiful
tapestries woven with pictures of
Jesus doing kind things: hugging
children, healing people, teaching.
Another tapestry showed cymbals,
mountains and bonfires. Around a
corner an arch was outlined in the
wall by stones. It surrounded a broad,
cross-shaped area with a hook in the
center. Scattered on the floor in front
of it were pieces of wood carved to
look like parts of a mannequin.
Each piece had a word written on

it—teaching, serving, giving . . .
Hanging on the walls and set in the
ground beside the arch were shields,
each emblazoned with a large cross.

"Weird!" Jamal muttered.

"This reminds me of Corinthians,"
Dad said. "Let's read."

Letter to the Corinthians–The Body

(1 Corinthians 12)

Paul started the church in Corinth on his second journey. Later the Corinthians disagreed with each other and wrote to Paul for help. He answered from the city of Ephesus, explaining that God wants the church to work like a body.

"There's one body with many parts. Suppose the foot says, 'I'm not a hand so I don't belong to the body.' It's still part of the body.

"If the whole body were an ear, how could it smell? God has placed

each part in the body just as he wanted it. If all the parts were the same, how could there be a body? As it is, there are many parts but one body.

"The head can't say to the feet, 'I don't need you!' In fact, the parts of the body that seem weaker are the ones we can't do without.

"God has joined together all the parts and given more honor to those that didn't have any. In that way, the parts of the body will take care of each other. If one part suffers, every part suffers with it. If one part is honored, every part shares its joy.

"You're the body of Christ. Each one of you is a part of it. You each have an important job to do."

Letter to the Corinthians–Love

(1 Corinthians 13; 2 Corinthians 5)

Paul wanted the Corinthians to understand how to live the Christian life. He wrote to explain what real love is.

"Suppose I speak in the languages of humans and angels. If I don't have love, I'm only a loud gong or noisy cymbal. Suppose I have the gift of prophecy, understand the secret things of God, and have enough faith to move mountains. If I don't have love, I'm nothing at all. Suppose I give everything I have to poor people. And suppose I give my body to be burned. If I don't have love, I get nothing at all.

"Love is patient. Love is kind. It doesn't want what belongs to others. It doesn't brag. It isn't proud or rude. It doesn't look out for its own interests. It doesn't easily become angry. It doesn't keep track of people's wrongs.

"Love isn't happy with evil. It's full of joy when truth is spoken. It always protects, always trusts, always hopes. It never gives up.

"Love never fails."

Paul knew that only Christians with God's Holy Spirit could love in this way. He wrote, "Anyone who believes in Christ is a new creation. The old is gone! The new has come!"

"Paul talked about a lot of stuff. What did he mean about clanging cymbals and mountains?" Jamal asked.

"He wanted us to know that *why* we do things is what matters," Mom explained. "Paul was saying that how much faith we have, or how spiritual we seem means nothing if we don't love people."

"What about all that stuff about the body?" Chris put in. "He meant the church, right?"

"Right. The church is important in helping us grow and in telling people about Jesus," Dad explained. "Everyone has a part to play. And all the parts are equally important."

Niki was examining the wooden pieces scattered on the floor. The largest looked like the chest part of a wooden mannequin. A heart shape was carved in the center of it. Within the heart was a cross, and at the center of the cross was a keyhole. "This is great! A cross in a heart. Like Jesus living in our hearts!" Niki exclaimed. "Is there a key for this?" They searched and eventually found one hanging on the wall beside the hook. It fit the hole but wouldn't turn.

"Let's put the body together," Chris suggested. "Like parts of the church. Cool! Hey! The main piece fits on the hook!" He hooked the torso-shaped piece onto the wall. They all worked to put the mannequin together. Simianne and Digger kept trying to help too. When it was done, the whole mannequin hung on the wall. They stepped back to admire their work.

"Jesus is the head of the church," Mom explained. "This mannequin represents the church. See," she pointed to the words on each piece, "different parts or people have different gifts and abilities."

"When everyone works together, the church is healthy," Dad added. "But if people fight over who's better or who's right, it's like a hand trying to be an ear."

They all laughed at the idea of a hand listening.

"Now try the key, Jamal," Chris suggested.

It turned! They heard the door they'd entered by close with a THUD. A door clicked open beside them. The small room behind it held armor and weapons.

"Are we supposed to wear this stuff?" Jamal asked putting the helmet on. It was huge on him.

"You know," Dad said slowly, "Paul wrote other letters to churches he'd started, to teach them about being Christians."

"But the armor?" the kids asked.

"That's what I'm talking about," Dad answered with a grin. "Your turn to read, Niki." He handed her the Bible.

What's Your Part?

There are many things you can do in the church: teach, encourage, greet, sing, pray, help others and tell people about Jesus. Look around.

God has prepared a job just for you. And it will be one that you're good at too. Get involved. Be a body part!

Verse: 1 Corinthians 12:18, 27

"God has placed each part in the body just as he wanted it to be . . . You are the body of Christ. Each one of you is a part of it."

Paul's Other Letters

(Ephesians 6; Philippians 2, 4)

Paul wrote letters to other churches too. He made sure they understood what Jesus had done, what it meant to their lives and how they should live. He wrote about freedom and joy even though he was a Roman prisoner when he wrote!

"Let the Lord make you strong. Put on all God's armor. Then you can stand firm against the devil's evil plans. Our fight isn't against humans. It's against the spiritual forces of evil in the heavenly world.

"Put on the belt of truth. Put the armor of godliness on your chest. Wear on your feet shoes that will prepare you to tell the good news of peace. Pick up the shield of faith to put out the flaming arrows of the evil one. Put on the helmet of salvation. And take the sword of the Spirit, God's word.

"At all times, pray by the power of the Spirit.

"Dear friends, continue to work out your own salvation. God is working in you. Always be joyful because you belong to the Lord! I'll say it again. Be joyful.

"Don't worry about anything. Instead, tell God about everything. Ask and pray. Give thanks to him. Then God's peace will watch over your hearts and minds because you belong to Christ Jesus."

Letters to Paul's Helpers

(1 Timothy 6; 2 Timothy 1–3; Titus 2)

Timothy and Titus helped Paul spread the news about Jesus. Paul loved them. He called Timothy his son. He carefully trained them to work in the churches. When he was old, Paul wrote letters to guide and encourage them:

"You gain a lot when you live a godly life. Try hard to do right. Have faith, love and gentleness. Hold on to what you believe. Fight the good fight along with other believers. Run from the evil things young people long for. We must control ourselves and lead godly lives in today's world. That's how we should live as we wait for Jesus Christ to appear.

"God didn't give us a spirit that makes us weak and fearful. He gave us a spirit that gives us power, love and self-control.

"Do your best to be a person who pleases God, a worker who doesn't need to be ashamed. Teach the message of truth correctly.

"You've known the Holy Scriptures since you were a child. They teach you how to be saved by believing in Christ Jesus. God has breathed life into all Scripture. It's useful for teaching what's true, correcting our mistakes, making our lives whole, and training us to do what's right. By using Scripture, God's people can be completely prepared to do every good thing."

"God promised the good news of Jesus would be for everyone," Dad said. "He used Paul and others to spread the news to people. And they had a lot of opposition!"

"From the Jews?" Niki guessed.

"And Romans," Dad said. "In fact, almost all the apostles were killed for following Jesus!"

"Where was the armor Paul talked about?" Jamal asked.

"Paul wasn't talking about metal and leather armor. He meant spiritual armor for fighting spiritual enemies," Dad explained. "Paul was saying God has given us everything we need to follow him and be safe from spiritual attack. Look." Dad brought the belt from the small armory. "Truth, like a belt, protects us from lies. Godliness or obeying God and becoming like Jesus protects us . . ."

"Like the breastplate!" Chris interrupted, getting the metal breastplate.

"Right!" Dad agreed with a smile. "Also, faith in God is a good shield from the enemy's arrows." He paused as Niki dragged the shield out into the hallway. "The Bible's like a sword for defending ourselves from Satan's attacks."

"Hey! Jesus used Scripture like that when he was tempted!" Jamal exclaimed, getting the sword.

"Exactly!" Mom replied. "Being ready to tell others about Jesus is like wearing the right shoes. And, finally, knowing we're saved protects our thoughts, like a helmet!"

"Let's protect this guy!" Chris suggested, grabbing the breastplate and putting it on the mannequin. Quickly they fit the rest of the armor on. As the last piece was put in place, the door to the armory closed with a CLUNK and another door farther down the hallway opened. Suddenly arrows shot out of the walls at them from all angles!

"Grab the shields!" Dad yelled, snatching one from against the wall. THWACK! Digger yelped, tucked his tail between his legs and raced for the open doorway! Everyone grabbed a shield for protection and sprinted for the safety of the door and the stairs beyond. But arrows shot from the stairway walls too. So they kept running until the thwacking against their shields stopped.

"That was wild!" Jamal shouted, grinning. Simianne screeched and jumped up and down on Jamal's head. Jamal tried to calm her as the group continued down the stairs to a small, stuffy room. It was bare except for a high backless stool standing before a tall desk. A reed pen, ink block, water jar and open parchment lay on the desk as if someone had just stepped away. Two smoky torches burned in brackets on the wall, casting flickering shadows.

"The apostles could have written their letters from somewhere like this," Mom said. "Let's rest and read." She handed the Bible to Jamal.

New Testament Writers

Others besides Paul wrote books in the New Testament. The disciple John wrote three letters, a gospel and Revelation. Matthew, the disciple, and Mark, an early believer, wrote gospels. Jude and James, Jesus' brothers, each wrote a letter. Peter wrote two letters. And Doctor Luke wrote a gospel and a history of the early church called Acts.

Verse: 2 Timothy 3:16-17

"God has breathed life into all of Scripture. It is useful for teaching us what is true. It is useful for correcting our mistakes. It is useful for making our lives whole again. It is useful for training us to do what is right. By using Scripture, God's people can be completely prepared to do every good thing."

James

(James 1–4)

Others besides the apostles were spreading the word about Jesus. James (Jesus' brother) was leading the Jerusalem church. During Paul's first journey James wrote to Jewish believers about how to live well.

"If you need wisdom, ask God for it. He gives freely to everyone. The wisdom that comes from heaven is pure. It loves peace, thinks about others and obeys. It's full of mercy and good fruit. It's fair.

"Don't just listen to the word and fool yourselves. Do what it says. What good is it if people claim they have faith but don't act like it? Faith without good works is dead.

"Ships are big. But they're steered by a small rudder. In the same way, the tongue is small. But no one can control the tongue. Suppose you think your beliefs are right because of how you live. But you don't control what you say. You're fooling yourselves. Your beliefs aren't worth anything at all. Everyone should be quick to listen, slow to speak, slow to get angry.

"'Love your neighbor as you love yourself.' If you really keep that law, you're doing what's right.

"Obey God. Stand up to the devil. He'll run away from you. Come near to God, and he'll come near to you."

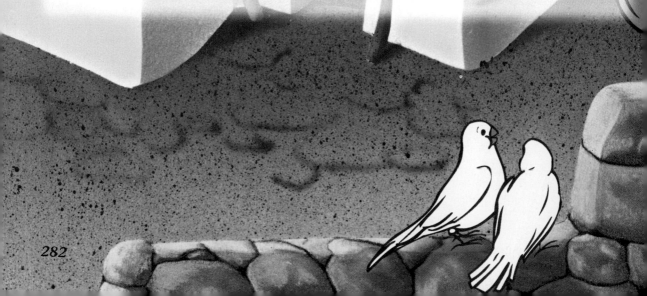

Peter

(1 Peter 1–2, 5)

Jesus forgave Peter for denying him during the trial.

Peter became one of the main leaders in the church. He preached and taught about Jesus to thousands. He was the first apostle to take the message to non-Jews. Later, Peter died for refusing to deny Jesus. He wrote:

"Through faith you're kept safe by God's power. Because you know this, you have great joy even though you may have had to suffer for a little while. Your troubles have come to prove your faith is real. It's worth more than gold.

"The blood of Christ set you free from an empty way of life. So get rid of every kind of evil. Stop telling lies. Don't pretend to be something you're not. Stop wanting what others have. Don't speak against each other.

"Like babies just born, long for the pure milk of God's word. It'll help you grow up as believers.

"Put on a spirit that's free of pride toward each other. Scripture says, 'God opposes those who are proud. But he gives grace to those who aren't.' Turn all your worries over to him. He cares about you.

"God always gives you all the grace you need."

John

(1 John 1, 3–5; 2 John)

John, the son of Zebedee, was also a strong leader in the church.
All the other disciples died before he did. He worked for many years in
Ephesus, perhaps with Paul's friend, Timothy. John was called "the
disciple Jesus loved." He wrote about love too:

"Dear friends, let's love one another, because love comes from God.
Everyone who loves has been born again and knows God. Anyone who
doesn't love doesn't know God, because God is love. What is love? It's not

that we loved God. It's that he loved us and sent his Son to give his life to pay for our sins.

"Dear friends, since God loved us that much, we should love one another. No one has ever seen God. But if we love one another, God lives in us.

"There's no fear in love. Instead, perfect love drives fear away. God is faithful and fair. If we admit that we've sinned, he'll forgive us our sins. He will make us pure.

"We love because he loved us first. The way we show our love is to obey God's commands. His commands aren't hard to obey. They're to believe in the name of his Son, Jesus Christ, and to love one another."

"James said God is even interested in our words!" Chris exclaimed.

Mom nodded. "What God says in the Bible, what you've been learning, has to work in everyday life. Most of the New Testament was written to teach us how to live."

"Good thing!" Chris said.

Dad smiled. "Uh-huh. And God's Spirit helps us. Jesus came to live in you. You're his temple, remember?" He looked around, "How do we get out of here?"

"Look at this!" Niki said, pointing to a fresco or wall painting. Several people were standing in a group holding hands and smiling. But the circle of people wasn't complete. One place was empty. "Someone's missing," she said, frowning.

"Here!" Jamal called. Across the room was a small fresco of one person standing in a meadow. "They should all be together," he guessed, "you know, loving one another and stuff." Chris and Jamal felt around the fresco. Suddenly a piece containing the person slid into their hands. They brought it across to the group. The person fit into the empty space perfectly!

KA-CHUNK! The wall the boys were leaning against suddenly opened. They tumbled through into a rough, dimly lit tunnel. A dusty, uneven path led downward past niches containing coffin-like stone boxes. Each niche had a plaque with the name of an apostle on it and the type of death he suffered.

"They were murdered!" Jamal exclaimed indignantly.

"Because they were Christians. They followed Christ even when it meant they had to die!" Dad explained.

"Wow!" the kids chorused. Digger barked along.

"What if someone said they'd kill you unless you denied Jesus?" Mom asked. "If kids made fun of you for being Christians, would you pretend not to believe in Jesus?"

The kids thought quietly for a moment. Finally, Chris said, "It would be tough, but I want to stick with Jesus." Niki and Jamal nodded emphatically.

The Spread of the Church

Amazing! It started with 12 men in Jerusalem and within 300 years Christianity had become the official religion of the Roman Empire! Now it's all over the world. People speaking hundreds of different languages worship God every week. And the church is still going to grow because God wants everyone to know him! Awesome!

Verse: James 1:22
"Don't just listen to the word. You fool yourselves if you do that. You must do what it says."

Mom smiled. "God helped the apostles stick with Jesus too. Every one of them suffered for believing in him."

The tunnel led them to an elaborate metal platform on the edge of a rocky outcropping halfway up the side of a huge cavern. Strange many-headed beasts were painted on the walls. Angels with trumpets stood on platforms around the cave. Far below, a small lake of burning oil covered part of the floor. Its acrid scent floated up to them. The rest of the floor was a beautiful, lush garden. A huge white throne stood between the burning lake and the garden.

"Check it out!" Jamal said. "This is out of a dream or something!"

"No," Dad smiled, "Revelation. Listen." He began to read.

The Last Judgment

(Revelation 12, 19–21)

John knew death wasn't the end of everything. He wrote about what would happen at the end of time:

"There was war in heaven. Michael and his angels fought against the dragon. But the dragon wasn't strong enough. The dragon, that old snake called the devil, or Satan, was thrown into the lake of burning sulphur.

"I saw heaven standing open. There in front of me was a white horse. Its rider is called Faithful and True. When he judges or makes war, he is always fair.

"I saw a great white throne and One sitting on it. I saw the dead, great and small, standing in front of the throne. Books were opened, including the Book of Life. The dead were judged by what they had done. The things they had done were written in the books. Anyone whose name wasn't written in the Book of Life was thrown into the lake of fire.

"I saw a new heaven and a new earth. It doesn't need the sun or moon. God's glory is its light, and the Lamb is its lamp. Only those whose names are written in the Lamb's Book of Life will enter the city."

Jesus' Return and Heaven

(Matthew 24; 1 Thessalonians 4; Revelation 21–22)

Jesus is preparing a place in heaven for his followers. No one can imagine how wonderful it will be!

Jesus said, "They'll see the Son of Man coming on the clouds of the sky. He'll come with power and great glory. He'll send his angels with a loud trumpet call. They'll gather his chosen people from all four directions."

We'll be caught up together with them, taken up in the clouds. We'll meet the Lord in the air. And we'll be with him forever.

A loud voice said, "Now God makes his home with human beings. They'll be his people. And God himself will be with them and be their God. He'll wipe away every tear. There'll be no more death or sadness, no more crying or pain."

The One on the throne said, "I'm making everything new! Anyone who is thirsty may drink from the spring of the water of life. It doesn't cost anything! Those who overcome will receive all this. I'll be their God, and they'll be my children. Look! I'm coming soon! I'll reward each of you for what you've done."

The Holy Spirit says, "Come!"

Let those who hear say, "Come!"

Amen. Come, Lord Jesus!

293

"That must be the dragon!" Jamal pointed to a beast on the wall.

"There's God's throne," Niki added. "And the lake for the dragon. Ugh!"

"It's for people whose names aren't in the Book of Life," Chris added. "How do people's names get into the book?"

"Well, God gave his only son," Mom began, "whoever believes in him . . ."

". . . won't die but will have eternal life!" the kids chorused.

"Exactly. Their names will be written in the Book of Life!" Mom concluded.

"Then our names are in it right now?" Jamal asked eagerly. Mom nodded.

"Cool! All right!" the kids shouted. Digger wagged his tail and Simianne clapped and chattered.

"At the judgment we'll go to heaven instead of the lake of fire," Dad said. "Heaven will be much more like that garden." They all looked at the garden for a minute. Brightly colored flowers dotted the areas between the lush green trees.

A trumpet blew. "What was that?" Chris asked.

"Hmm. That must be the angel's trumpet call before Jesus' return," Mom guessed. They all held their breath, waiting for something to happen.

At last Jamal suggested, "There are seven angels here. Maybe they all have to blow their trumpets."

"You're right!" Dad agreed excitedly. "Revelation also talks about seven angels blowing trumpets as God completes everything." Just then another trumpet blew. Dad grinned at Jamal. "You were right!"

Every couple minutes, as they talked, another trumpet sounded.

"This cavern represents the end of God's plan," Mom said thoughtfully. "We have him with us in our hearts now. Then we'll also be with him in heaven!"

"That's his whole plan, huh?" Chris asked. "That's why Jesus died for us."

Niki added excitedly, "Because we're his treasure!"

Mom gave Niki a hug. "Exactly. Our job is to believe, obey and tell others." She pointed to the fire. "Some people choose not to believe. They reject God and his love and forgiveness. They're sent to the lake of fire called hell. People who believe will live forever with God in heaven."

"Will that happen soon?" Jamal asked.

"When God's ready," Dad replied. "How many trumpets have blown?"

"Six," Chris answered.

"When the seventh goes . . . ," Dad began. But the seventh trumpet interrupted him. Suddenly the platform they were standing on started rising!

"What's happening?" Niki asked, peeling Simianne off her neck.

"Remember what we read? We'll meet Jesus in the air!" Dad said. "One day this will be for real!"

Heaven

Heaven's going to be a great place! The best thing about Heaven is that we'll be with God there. Lots of great things come with that. And all the things that make life hard will be missing! No pain or sorrow, crying or sickness, sadness or death. Hey, that sounds like . . . heaven!

Verse: Philippians 3:8
"Even more, I consider everything to be nothing compared to knowing Christ Jesus my Lord. To know him is the best thing of all. Because of him I have lost everything. But I consider all of it to be garbage so I can get to know Christ."

The platform continued to rise. Suddenly it stopped with a CLUNK! The group stepped out into a small, square room high in one of the castle towers. Two walls were wide open to the outside and gave a breathtaking view of the surrounding countryside. Wind whistled through the tower carrying scents of soil, flowers and fresh air. While the group excitedly pointed things out to each other, a door behind them opened silently. Zareef stepped through with a big smile. "May I have the Treasure Bible, please?" he grinned, holding out his hand.

Everyone jumped. "Wha . . . ? You knew the whole time!" Chris exclaimed.

"Of course, yes," Zareef smiled. "It is my job. I am the castle caretaker."

"You set us up with the map," Mom guessed. "You had the pieces all along!"

Zareef nodded, "But it was more interesting this way, yes?"

Dad laughed as he handed Zareef the Bible. "Yes! We enjoyed the search and the finding. I take it these really are Tresor's Caverns?"

Zareef nodded. He led them through the door he'd used, down winding stairs to the pedestal room and returned the Treasure Bible to the column. "Long ago Tresor decided to study the Bible in a physical way. He wanted to learn how it fit together, to discover the main threads of God's plan. He and friends, skilled workers and artists, built this place with many ingenious devices. All teach God's Word and God's plan."

"We learned an awful lot!" Niki said. The others nodded in agreement. Simianne chattered her opinion and Digger barked his too. The adults laughed.

"You certainly understand the Bible more than when we came!" Dad agreed.

"And," Jamal added, "we found the treasure of God. Us!"

"Exactly!" Zareef waved his arms. "Excellent! That is why this castle is here!" He grinned. "It is a way for those who truly seek God to find him."

"We *have* to tell people about this place!" the kids declared.

"Yes! Good! Tell them what you have learned. People must hear about God's plan. Tresor's purpose was to make the Bible come alive through this castle."

"We prayed this trip would get the kids excited about God's Word," Mom said. "It sure worked! Thanks!"

Zareef retrieved three books from behind the column. "Here are Treasure Bibles for you," he said, handing them to the kids. "These are easier to carry than the one you used here, yes? Never forget what you learned here. Keep reading God's Book and you will continue to solve mysteries and find adventures."

"For us? Wow! Thanks, Zareef!" the kids cried in amazement, taking the Bibles. They opened them eagerly and began to read.

Going to Church

As Christians there are many reasons for going to church. In church we learn to love and encourage one another as Christians. We receive good teaching about God and how to live. And we grow in our own love and worship of God. The list goes on . . .

Verse: Revelation 22:20
"He who gives witness to these things says, 'Yes. I am coming soon.' Amen. Come, Lord Jesus!"

299

Treasure's task now begun, obedience to the Coming One.

How to Use the Amazing Treasure Bible

The *Amazing Treasure Bible* was written especially for you! If you read this book from cover to cover, you'll begin to understand God's reason for writing all the stories and lessons in the Bible.

The *Amazing Treasure Bible* includes Bible stories taken right from the Bible. These stories will lead you through God's plan for all of us, from creation through Revelation. Woven between the Bible stories is an exciting adventure story that will help you learn important Biblical truths.

The *Amazing Treasure Bible* connects all the many Bible stories into one whole story. It will help you understand God's purpose and will tell you how you can be close to him. As you read it, you'll get excited, and you'll want to read more and more. But even more than that—we hope you'll get to know the God this book is all about. He loves you and his plan is for you too, not just the people in the stories.

You can use this book in many ways:

1. You can read it on your own and learn with the kids in the story—Chris, Jamal and Niki.

2. You can read it with your parents. You can read it with your brothers and sisters, if you have any. Or you can read it with your friends. The *Amazing Treasure Bible* has two or three Bible stories followed by stories about Chris, Jamal and Niki. They talk about the Bible stories and solve clues. You can easily read one section (Bible stories and discussion) in one sitting. It's perfect for family devotions!

3. Maybe your parents will want to read ahead and help you solve the clues as you go. You can read the stories together then discuss everything that happens and what it means.

4. Chris, Jamal and Niki learn things and ask questions. You can too! Instead of reading their answers, think about the answers for yourself!

Index & Dictionary

There are some hard words in this book that you might not know. Here are simple meanings for the important words and where you can read about them. Sometimes you'll find the words in the special notes on a page. These notes are separated from the rest of the page by lines.

blood–the liquid in our bodies that keeps us alive; it's needed for forgiveness 70, 77, 225-229

–Jesus' 227-229, 285

born again–saved from sins; see also *salvation*..219, 250

C

Caesar–ruler of the Roman empire.......170, 174

Cain–Adam and Eve's son who killed his brother, Abel....................................36-37

Caleb–one of Joshua's 12 spies 85

children/kids–young people, also someone's descendants........................100, 222-223

–of Abraham 45-47

–of God 30, 266, 293

Christ–name of the Messiah who God promised would help all nations, a title for Jesus 176-179, 220, 232, 266

church–a place where Christians meet 248-249, 258, 270-271, 274-275, 288, 297

command–an instruction or order that should be obeyed....................................143, 263

–God's 79, 287

–the greatest commandment 206, 203

–the Ten Commandments 82-83

Corinthians–letters written by Paul to Christians in the city of Corinth 270-273

Cornelius–a Roman commander Peter told about Jesus, the first non-Jewish Christian 252, 261

covenant–a serious agreement between two people or between God and people.....225

–David with Jonathan...............................110

–God with Abraham 45

–God with Noah 39

–new covenant, God with all people........149, 225-229

–old covenant, God with Moses and the Israelites.......................79, 129, 143, 225

creation–making something out of nothing...27, 29-30, 273

crucifixion/crucify–a way to kill people by nailing them to a wooden cross 232

D

Daniel–an Israelite leader in Babylon who obeyed God faithfully 154-158

David–king of Israel who obeyed God, ancestor of Jesus 109-122, 126, 174, 220

Deborah–a leader of Israel............................92

desert–a dry area where little grows 85-87

–Jesus is led there 188

–where God appears to Moses...................64

–where John the Baptist preached...........187

devil–an evil angel who is God's enemy 188, 208, 277

–he is defeated 290

–he will flee 282

die/death–to stop living, physical or spiritual..............................42-43, 293-295

–a result of sin 30, 33, 39, 43

–Jesus' 228-229, 232-235

–part of the Passover 77

disciples–followers of Jesus, 12 men Jesus chose 192-197, 222-223, 231, 236-237

disobey–to refuse to obey or follow

–examples 33, 42, 105

307

Scripture Index

You might want to know where to find a certain Bible verse or chapter in this book. Here is a list of the books of the Bible and chapters from them that we have used. The page numbers where you'll find them are given here too.

A verse that is marked with a star (for example *1:1) means that verse is a memory verse. You'll find it beside the notes on a page, separated from the main part of the page by lines.

A page number in brackets (for example [124]) means you'll find that Bible reference in the notes on that page. The notes are with the memory verses, separated from the main part of the page by lines.

Castle Floor Plans

Level one

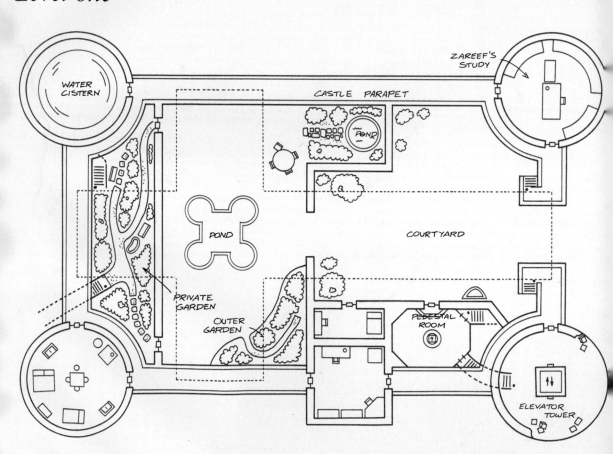

ZAREEF'S STUDY

WATER CISTERN

CASTLE PARAPET

POND

POND

COURTYARD

PRIVATE GARDEN

OUTER GARDEN

PEDESTAL ROOM

ELEVATOR TOWER

Level two

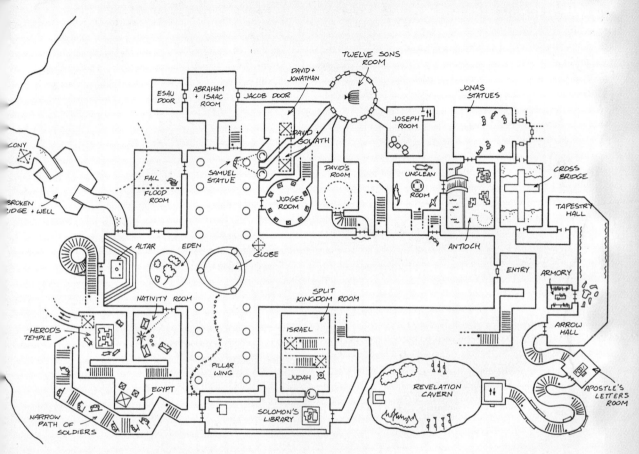

ESAU DOOR

ABRAHAM + ISAAC ROOM

JACOB DOOR

DAVID + JONATHAN

TWELVE SONS ROOM

JONAS STATUES

JOSEPH ROOM

BALCONY

BROKEN BRIDGE + WELL

FALL FLOOD ROOM

SAMUEL STATUE

DAVID + GOLIATH

DAVID'S ROOM

UNCLEAN ROOM

CROSS BRIDGE

JUDGES ROOM

GLOBE

ANTIOCH

TAPESTRY HALL

ALTAR

EDEN

SPLIT KINGDOM ROOM

ENTRY

ARMORY

NATIVITY ROOM

ISRAEL

ARROW HALL

HEROD'S TEMPLE

JUDAH

REVELATION CAVERN

APOSTLE'S LETTERS ROOM

PILLAR WING

EGYPT

NARROW PATH OF SOLDIERS

SOLOMON'S LIBRARY

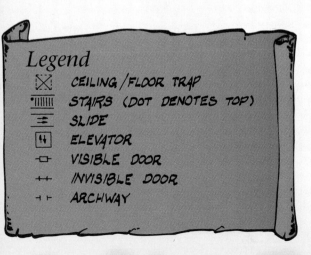

Legend

⊠	CEILING/FLOOR TRAP
·⊪⊪⊪	STAIRS (DOT DENOTES TOP)
⇌	SLIDE
⊞	ELEVATOR
⊐	VISIBLE DOOR
++	INVISIBLE DOOR
⊢⊣	ARCHWAY

Level three

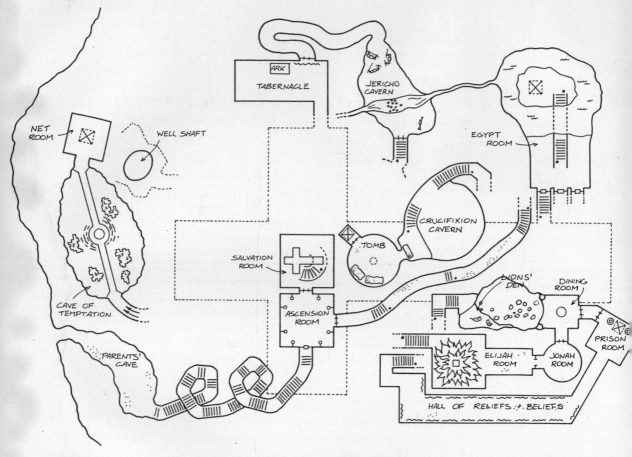

NET ROOM

WELL SHAFT

TABERNACLE

ARK

JERICHO CAVERN

EGYPT ROOM

CAVE OF TEMPTATION

SALVATION ROOM

CRUCIFIXION CAVERN

TOMB

LIONS' DEN

DINING ROOM

PARENTS' CAVE

ASCENSION ROOM

PRISON ROOM

SLIDE

ELIJAH ROOM

JONAH ROOM

HALL OF RELIEFS + BELIEFS

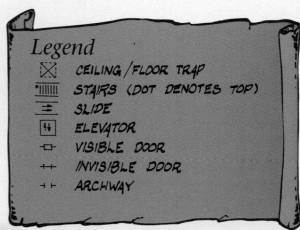

Legend

⊠	CEILING/FLOOR TRAP
▪‖‖‖	STAIRS (DOT DENOTES TOP)
⇌	SLIDE
⊞	ELEVATOR
⊏⊐	VISIBLE DOOR
++	INVISIBLE DOOR
⊢ ⊣	ARCHWAY

Lightwave Publishing Inc.

Lightwave's mission is to develop quality resources and related services that encourage, assist and equip parents to build Christian faith with their children.

Lightwave's learning resources have been sold or endorsed by such ministries as *Josh McDowell Ministry, Campus Crusade for Christ, Christian Financial Concepts, The 700 Club, Living Way Ministries* and *The American Family Association.*

Rick and Elaine Osborne

Rick Osborne, author and speaker, encourages and teaches parents to pass on Christian faith to their children. He is the founder and president of Lightwave Publishing and Lightwave Kids Club.

Since 1984, Rick and his wife Elaine have been developing and producing high quality materials that help parents teach their children about God and the Bible. Among the more than 30 books and resources are *101 Questions Children Ask About God, The Singing Bible, Sticky Situations (the McGee and Me Game),* and *The Adventure Bible Handbook.* Rick recently co-authored a book with Larry Burkett entitled *Financial Parenting.*

Tips & Tools

Lightwave offers a free bi-monthly newsletter called *Tips & Tools for Spiritual Parenting.* This newsletter helps parents make church exciting for their kids, helps them answer their kids' questions, and helps them teach their children to pray. It also provides ideas for fun activities and much more. To receive a free one year subscription, simply write to the address below to request it or call **1-800-555-9884.**

Lightwave Publishing Inc.
133, 800 - 5th Ave.,
Suite 101,
Seattle, WA
98104-3191

or, in Canada,
Lightwave Publishing Inc.
Box 160
Maple Ridge, B.C.
Canada V2X 7G1

You and your children can also visit Lightwave's Internet site at www.beacom.com/lw.

Lightwave Publishing does not accept or solicit donations.

God sees you as a treasure, the same way he saw the kids in this story as a treasure.

Jesus died for you. You can pray and tell God you believe in what Jesus did. You can accept Jesus' sacrifice for you and live forever with him by praying this prayer:

"Dear God, I know I'm a sinner. I have made wrong choices and done bad things. I'm sorry. Please forgive me. I know your Son, Jesus, died for my sins. I believe you raised him from the dead and that he is Lord. I accept what he did for me. Help me trust and obey you and make right choices. I want to be your child. Thank you for loving me and seeing me as your treasure. Thanks for living in me. In Jesus' name, amen."

To help yourself never forget this important decision, sign in the space below.

I, _____ , accepted Jesus today.

I became a child of God. Date: _____

To grow as a Christian, here are some things you should do:

* Pray. Talk to God from your heart about anything, anytime, anywhere.

* Get a complete Bible and begin reading it. It has even more exciting stories than this one. You might start with Mark, then read Acts or James. Then read Genesis. See if you can see God's big plan in the stories you read.

* Tell your friends about what has happened to you. They can become God's children too.

* Find a local church where they love Jesus and teach the Bible. You'll meet more of God's children and learn about God.